Road Map
to
Life

WALTER BERNARD WARD SR.

Fulton Books, Inc.
Meadville, PA

Published by Fulton Books 2020

ISBN 978-1-64654-377-9 (paperback)
ISBN 978-1-64654-378-6 (digital)

Printed in the United States of America

A Life in Somerset County

I am a man that was born, 1952 in Somerset County, Maryland. As I grew up, I saw many things happen in life. Some things I understood as well as many I didn't. Some things I saw, and I thought they were good. Later, I found out they were not. I saw White men coming to my house, laughing and talking to my father, his brothers, and their parents. Once I got older, I found out that the money my family was giving to these men was a legal robbery. They were collecting insurance money. Our families felt that this money was payment for their burial when they died.

As I look back, our families were only filling the pockets of the insurance companies. After paying their money for all their lives, when they finally passed away, there wasn't enough money to bury them. The remainder of the family still had to come up with most of the money for the undertaker to bury them. I am so glad that I grew up with my father as well as my uncles. They were very close, and we found ourselves together almost every day.

At these times, I didn't hear talk of running women, fighting, drinking, or other negative things. I was always privy to hear positive talk about current events. These things about life have helped me all through my life, even until today. In those days, children were seen and not heard until asked. I learned a lot, and later, I was allowed to join the conversations. These were the days of the freedom fighting. I heard about Rosa Parks as a child, though I didn't understand the full magnitude of what she did.

As I think back, I can understand the meaning of Dr. King and all the people that were called communist. I realized early that anyone that was Black and spoke up against White people were bad and considered communist. Even the uneducated Blacks thought that the freedom fighters were wrong. I realized that the White men were able to convince the poor Blacks that what was being done was bad for society.

I heard my uncle say once, "Tell some, but keep some." When I got to junior high, I learned firsthand what that meant. My uncle was telling his parents and brothers an experience he'd had. He was working in a crab house. He had worked for this company for many years since before the owner's children were born. He had been there so long they made him the "boss."

Every day when my uncle got to work, he checked in with the owner. He would say, "We doing the same thing today, boss?" referring to him still running the operation. One day, he went in as usual, and the boss told him that he had hired someone and he wanted him to follow my uncle around. He told my uncle to "show him the ropes." The man followed my uncle around for almost a year. This took so long because this was a massive operation. They processed crabs, oysters, and soft crabs. They also handled the shipping and receiving at that plant. My uncle knew the whole operation. I guess this was too much for a Black man to know all about this White man's business. The boss could have gone on vacation for a month and his business would have been run as if he had never left. My uncle could run the company and was still making the boss a lot of money, but I guess this was a case of a Black man being too smart, or (as the White men called it) being an "uppity" nigger.

One day, my uncle went to work and went through the usual routine. "We doing the same thing today, boss?" But this day, the boss told him, "Talk to the man, he'll tell you what to do." My uncle had trained a White man to take his job! That's why he said "Tell some, but leave some." I vowed from that moment never to train anyone for anything! Not only did I make sure I taught it to my sons, I taught it to every Black person who would listen.

My parents, as well as most of the family that were older, were educated, and the ones that were not listened and took examples from the ones that were. My great-grandfather owned land and sold land to others. He had Black and White people working for him. We were never a family that allowed anyone to do anything to us because they thought they were better than us. From learning as a child that no one was better than me, that we were all equal, helped me when I was a senior in high school.

That was the first year of total integration over the whole county. I had gone to an all-Black school for eleven years. Now in the school year '69–'70, I found myself in a mixed school for the first time ever. Let me tell you a few stories about that! I played sports, and I realized that the White children loved to be around the Black athletes. There were a few White boys that hung around me. One day during the basketball season, as we were walking down the hall, a group of White girls were walking toward us. (I don't know if this was planned before hand or not.) As we got closer, one of the boys said, "When these girls get closer, I'm going to kick you in the ass. But don't do anything." I said, "What did you say?" He repeated himself and added that he wanted his girlfriend to think that he was superior to me. Well, I said to him, "Call the police and the ambulance 'cause you may be dead if you kick me!" I don't care how many White boys were with me and that I was the only Black boy in the hall. I was not afraid! I knew I could beat all of them alone. Needless to say, I didn't get kicked!

The principal of the school, whenever there was a racial problem in the school, would call me and ask me to mediate. During these times, there were lots of racial issues to address. The Blacks were not happy about being taken from our comfort zone, and the White felt that they were superior and now the niggers were coming to their school!

When I was in the all-Black school, we had discipline, children learning, and a whole lot less disrespect. We had doctors, lawyers, dentists, preachers, and teachers coming out of the Black schools before integration. In fact, there were more Black professionals to graduate from our schools than there have been since integration.

When we walked into the integrated schools, we found things worse than they were while we were in our schools. When we were in our schools, all of our teachers were professional and were teaching in their field of study. They had all graduated from college and were certified. When we got to the integrated school, the teachers didn't even need to have a degree, let alone a certification in the field they were teaching in. It was rare to have a teacher who had even finished four years of college. Most of the teachers were relatives or friends of teachers who had retired.

A Black teacher could not get a job teaching unless we had not only graduated but also passed the National Teacher's Examination. That's why we had teachers from many parts of the country in our local schools. In the Black schools, we were taught pride, respect, hard work, and discipline. We were taught that no one gives you anything, you have to work for it, and even then it is very hard. We were given history to know who we are.

Once we went to the White schools, we lost all these attributes. At our schools, we were used to coming into the classroom quietly and waiting for the bell to ring so we can have devotions. We would salute the flag, read scripture, pray and have news, and sing some songs. This was done daily from first to 12th grade. It helped calm us down and get them prepared for the day.

When I walked into the school, none of this was done. When the bell rang to start the day, we found our seats and waited quietly for devotions to start. I can remember getting so scared when I looked around and saw all the White students walking around playing and talking. It was still a warm day in September, and some of the White children were sitting on the windowsills hollering out to the people walking by the school.

I can still see my homeroom teacher trying to take roll and the White students answering for each other whether they are present or not. The White students were calling the teacher by their first name or a nickname. I would go home and tell my father and his family what was going on in the school. They said, "This is going to be trouble later." As the Black students watched the White students and the way they behaved with no recourse, we started to do the same.

This wasn't as prevalent in the high school grades. We had years of training in the all-Black school system. However, as time went on, the younger children in their classes began to follow the examples

6

of the White children in their classrooms. They began to call the teacher by their first name and be disrespectful in other ways as well. It wasn't long before these bad habits started to rear their ugly heads in the homes as well. For the first time, in a lot of homes, little Black children were beginning to disrespect their parents. They had witnessed this in the schools with the White children interacting with their parents.

When these same White parents who were being disrespected by their children saw the behavior of the Black children (before they were corrupted), they came up with the idea that parents were not allowed to spank their children. The White people who made the laws started the law that teachers and principals could not spank children. This was because the White parents didn't want a Black teacher having to reprimand their child. Now, we have Black children in their homes telling their parents that they will call the cops on them for trying to discipline them. After all this, all discipline, respect, and everything was out the window. The children are now in control.

When I started to teach in 1976, I remembered the principal calling a White parent to school as her son was being very bad in school again. She came to the school about her child. I was on the planning period, so the principal (who was a Black lady) asked me to come to the office to help with the boy. The boy was in the 2nd grade. I was the phys ed teacher at the school. While we were in the office, the teacher was telling the mother what her son was doing. The mother said something to the boy, and then she spanked him. The boy was small, and he moved a chair over to his mother, stood in it, and slapped his mother in the face! She just dropped her head and cried. She then said, "Whatever you need to do to my child when he acts up, do it!" Now, who Black was going to do anything to this boy but send him home? We all know that if we had hit that child, the parents would have put the law on us and we would be in trouble. All discipline is gone from the schools now.

Now, let's get back to the community. When I was growing up, Marion and Crisfield were prosperous places. This may be true of many communities, but I can only speak of mine. There were many farms owned by both Blacks and Whites. The area was well-known

7

over the county for its productions. The rules for the federal government stopped the farms. The officials in Annapolis and Washington put the rules and regulations on the farmers without ever coming to the area to know what was going on so great that they put the farmers out of business. Even if the information they based the laws on were true, they should have done more investigation into the matter before making such harsh rules.

In the summer, I worked at the employment office in Somerset County as a liaison between the farmers and the migrant workers. My job was through the employment office, but my supervision was from Washington and his supervision was from Philadelphia. Neither of these men knew anything about the farms in Somerset County. Still, they made the rules. The only thing that they knew about the farms of Somerset County was what I would tell them. I was a college graduate, and I was aware of these facts, so I could tell them whatever I wanted. This kept my job though I was trying to help the farmers, the officials would still do what they wanted.

In Crisfield, the city was run by the mayor and city council. All of these people were the owners of the seafood packing houses. Crisfield was in the encyclopedia as the seafood capital of the world. There were more various seafoods coming from Crisfield than any place in the world. However, this fact in the encyclopedia has put Crisfield where it is today, which is a ghost town. When I was growing up, there were over ten thousand people in the area. If this is not true, then the officials of Crisfield lied as there was a sign or billboard along the highway that read WELCOME TO CRISFIELD, A WHOLESOME CITY. At that time, there were movie theaters, bowling alleys, teenage places, good stores, and many other things going on that made home a visitors' attraction.

There were businesses that wanted to come to Crisfield because it was growing so much and that they could transport their products up and down the waterways for much cheaper than on land. This did not happen as the city officials owned the seafood industry and blocked any competition. They had a monopoly on the workers of the city. Let me say this, the officials had a legal slave area. This was not to the Blacks only, but the White people who felt that they were superior were also slaves.

Why would I say that? I'm glad you asked. Now, let me tell you…

Those seafood packers had all become millionaires. Some of their family members were well-off as well. But as time has gone on, where are these millionaires and their families now? The millionaires are dead, and their relatives have had to move away from Crisfield just like the Blacks. All the officials from before the '50s–'80s lined their pockets gathering all the money for themselves. They did not have any vision or love for the future of the city at all. You, White people of today, are trying to get angry with Black people and even still think you are superior to the Blacks. Well, guess what? Your forefathers didn't care about you either! You were slaves and mistreated by the rich White people as well. They gave you White people a slightly better job than the Blacks, but you are still not on their level. You are labeled a "useless feeder" just like us. Unless you were one of the relatives of the millionaires before, you are one of the have-nots as well. The officials made you slaves too. If that's not true, explain to me why your relatives had to leave Crisfield and Marion just like the Blacks. There were no jobs for you either.

Now, let me break down what I am saying. Those crab packers had the watermen to bring the crabs, oysters, and soft crabs in. There were also fish and clams harvested. All of you, White people, had the jobs managing the crab houses. Your wives didn't work as pickers as the packers were paying you so much money that they didn't have to work. In those days, White people could buy homes, cars, and anything else. But only had to pay the interest on the products. The White girls or women had the jobs as stereotypes or would go to college for a few years and then be given jobs as teachers of White students. At the time, there were two elementary schools in Crisfield and one high school. This made more jobs for the White women. This was true whether there were enough qualified teachers or not. From the "good ol' boy" system, this was allowed to happen.

When schools integrated, it had to stop for a while until they were able to get the right people in positions to keep it going. In this way, the White women didn't have to do any dirty work. They became teachers, store clerks, bank tellers, and all other positions of clean work. The Black women had to become crab pickers, oyster shuckers, and all the other dirty work jobs. The Black men had to go in the field and all the hard work jobs. One time, you, readers, may not know, it was a death sentence by hanging if a Black person could read. As long as the Blacks stayed uneducated, they could control our minds as well as our bodies. As long as the White man could keep the Blacks and poor White trash under foot, the rich could control all. The rich White industry leaders left no money in the cities, except what they left to their families. Even the Whites that were allowed to feel that they were superior to us but they were in the same state Blacks were in.

Let's go in another direction for a while. There had always been money sent into Somerset County from the state and federal government. This was done as the officials had found ways to keep this very prosperous town in poverty. On top of being the ones keeping the citizens in poverty, they also kept all the money that was sent in for themselves. The citizens never benefited from it, or even knew when it came in. I am trying to make the people of the area to realize that they are fighting against each other, when the working class people, both Black and White, we are all being cheated by the people that are controlling the city government.

As my brothers and I have spoken to the state officials in Annapolis concerning the plight of the people in Crisfield, we have been told that government money come in every year. They tell the officials that all money that is not used per year is to be sent back to the state. People of Somerset County, where is the money? I am asking everyone, regardless of the color of your skin.

Every year, the area hosted the Crab Derby. At one time, there was a lot of money made for the city during this weekend. Where does all that money go? Now, the Crab Derby is not as great as it was years ago. This is true as not as many people come to town or home as there is nothing to do.

When I was growing up in Crisfield, I heard that each year, there was a chairman, and his or her (usually his) staff was in charge of the crab derby. We always heard that the chairman would change yearly as it was that person's turn to get a cut of the money. Is that true? I don't know, but I will say that there were no improvements made to the city as a result.

I remember in the '80s there was also a bluegrass festival in Crisfield. The city rented about twenty BO buses for some place to transport the people to and from the festival. This festival was held over on Jersey Island. It was said by some White people that there was over 250k made from the festival. This was allegedly after all expenses had been paid for the occasion. But no one ever saw any of that money either. Citizens of Somerset County, where did that money go? When I ask these questions, or say anything about Crisfield, Marion, or the school system, I am labeled a troublemaker.

Well, they can call me a troublemaker or whatever label they want to put on me. There's a chance that after writing this book, I may be killed or blackballed again, but I am asking questions to get at the truth. Nothing that I have said or will say in this book is a lie. If you will read, study, and research the things that I am saying, you will know that I am telling the truth. The reason I've decided to write this book at this time is that now is the time and this is the only way this information will get out.

I've tried to write articles to the local papers. Some were printed, some were not. One of those articles was in regards to Crisfield High School. This article was concerning access to the school gym as there were young men who wanted to use it on Saturdays from 10:00 a.m. to 1:00 p.m. Let me tell you that back in the '70s and '80s, we wanted to play on the weekends but were not allowed to. The Black men who had graduated from Crisfield High, and are now paying taxes in the area, wanted to use the gym. Most of us had played for the school team during our time there. However, we would go to the school and see the White men from Crisfield, Marion, and Salisbury playing. When we would walk in and try to play, they would stop playing, put their clothes on, and say that they were finished playing. When they left, they would lock the gym up and leave. The crazy thing that we would notice was that once we left, they would come back and open the gym back up.

That was then, I was just hoping that we had made some progress. It was now 2006 at the time I wrote the article. The difference in this situation was that I had gotten permission from the principal as well as the Board of Education. We went into the gym for about five Saturdays with no problem. The newspaper even sent someone to watch. There was sometimes forty or fifty men and boys in the back gym. We played cross court so that we could play two games at the same time. We even had the younger boys playing in the back gym. The reporter took pictures and put it in the paper. He gave us praise, and everything was going well.

Later, we got comments from people in top positions to state why we had to stop playing. For none of the reasons that they said we had to stop playing did they have a problem with us. Every reason that they came up with had nothing to do with what was going on on the school property. They said that some food had been stolen from the cafeteria. This happened during the school week, not on Saturday. They said that there was graffiti on the building. When they found the culprits, it had nothing to do with our Saturday basketball time. The next thing they said was that some lights had been broken on the outside. Once again, this was found to not have happened while we were there.

Finally, they said that we couldn't play anymore. That was that. I wrote an article and gave it to the editor of the *Crisfield Times*. This paper was printed once a week. In the past, anyone that wrote an article would have their article posted one week, and if anyone wanted to comment, they would post them the following week. Well, guess what? Instead of the editor following business as usual and posting my article as it was written, he edited it and allowed the board to read it before it was posted. He then went on to post their rebuttal to my article in the same paper. Right beside mine! This was unheard of! My prior issues with trying to get this information out is why I'm writing this now. Perhaps someone may respond, but all of what I have to say will be said. This is important because everything I'm saying is the truth.

Let's get back to growing up in the lower Somerset County area. I know that many of you are waiting for me to talk about what happened to me as a teacher in Somerset County. That's another story for another time. What I want to talk about now is the money situation there. My main question is where is the money that comes in? Why is Crisfield dying instead of moving forward? Let's look at the center on the corner of Fourth and Cove St. There was a lot more money put in for that center when it was built, but all the money that was given for it didn't go to that center. That basketball court or gym was outdated when it was built. There were no bleachers put around the court, and the basketball court was tile. The whole court is only the size of a half court, and there were no locker rooms. This center was a disgrace from the time it was built, and there was never any work done to it since.

The building has been there for over fifteen years now, and now it's falling apart. The building is sinking and the tiles are breaking up. There is only three thousand dollars given to the person to operate the building. This is supposed to service over one hundred children and even more men and women. But Black people have always been able to make a lot happen with a little bit of money.

I asked the mayor for a swimming pool in the city. He said that it was in the twenty-five-year plan for Crisfield. Well, guess what? What about the children of today? I have always been told that an idle mind is the devil's playground. The young people of Crisfield don't have anything to do after school or during the summer. There is no recreation for the children. But guess what? The town gets the grants from the government to say that they need money as Crisfield is a poverty-stricken area and because it is gang infested. They also get the money to combat the drug problems in the area. I say to both the Black and White citizens of Crisfield, where is the money? None of it goes back to the state. Then why don't we see the results of the money? One thing we all know is that we don't see improvements in the town.

Let me also say this while it's on my mind. The town received almost thirty million dollars from the government after Hurricane Sandy. Where is that money? It has been almost two years at the time of this writing, and where is that money? How much of it is left? We are beginning to see some homes go up, but is that even the Sandy money? Everyone that I have heard talk about their home, their insurance is paying for their homes. It was in the paper over the country that the lady's home behind number 1 school was the result of the money given for hurricane relief. Well let me tell you, none of that money was from the government. Her husband had flood insurance, and the labor was free from the people coming to the area that put her home up. Where is the Sandy money?

I was told that they people that are in charge of the Sandy money went on a trip to Tangier or Smith Island to check those places out. That trip allegedly cost over 10k. Let me tell you, people, none of you are on the board to watch how that money is being spent. I'm a troublemaker because I am telling you that you need to start to watch and ask questions. The money came to Crisfield for your benefit, but none of you know how it's being spent. The people that knew where the money is are not from Crisfield, and if they are, they are the people that have and not, you everyday people, the have-nots.

Just as the old officials from years gone by always kept the Blacks and Whites fighting with each other, the powers that be are doing the same thing to you citizens of today. As long as they can keep us at odds with each other, you can't be watching what they are doing. Look at the mayor, he is leaving office and running for state office. He said that there is nothing to gain in Crisfield as it is too crooked.

If you, people, would come together as other cities are doing, Crisfield and Marion could grow. While you are fighting and not working together, you can't see that there are less and less people in the area. The young people of childbearing age are leaving, and their children are growing up in other areas. The numbers in the schools are declining. You, people, did everything you could a few years ago to keep Crisfield High open. You are not looking at the thing that is happening. If you, people in this area, don't stop fighting each other, you're going to lose your school anyway as there are not enough children in the school to keep it open. If people of the lower Somerset County need to come together and force the city council and the county commissioners to bring jobs to the area, you're going to hear the superintendent of schools and the Board of Education saying that they are going to have to close the high school.

There have been opportunities to have jobs come to the area lately, but the officials are continuing to keep the jobs out and forcing the young people to leave the area to raise their children. Just a few years ago, the western shore wanted to start a ferry from the DC area to Crisfield. This ferry would have transported 100–200 car per trip, and it would have come to Crisfield. If that had been allowed to happen, there would have been the need for jobs, restaurants, hotels, and other types of businesses there. This would have kept the young families in the area, and the area would be booming right now instead of a ghost town. Then Wal-Mart wanted to put their hub warehouse in Somerset County as this is the central area for all their stores from upper Maryland, Delaware, and Virginia. This would have brought over six hundred jobs to the area.

As I travel to the various communities, I see the adults of all races working together to train their children in sports, they have little children on mixed teams of basketball, football, soccer, and all other kinds of sports. The other areas are working together to make their school teams better. There is a lot of talent in this area. However, the talent is working as separate teams. If the Black and White teams would come together, you could compete and beat other teams from anywhere. That little center at the end of south Fourth St. is taking the boys and girls to Fruitland to compete in activities there. When they go up there, they become the best at whatever sport they play. Why don't we come together in lower Somerset County work together and have the sports there so they can travel to other places and represent where they're from and win? All other areas are coming together, and this is the year 2019. Crisfield and Marion are still trying to act like it's the '50s and '60s.

There was a football team back in the '50s as I have been told in Crisfield. I heard that Bud Coulbourne's son was playing, and he died during a game. A mandate was made then that there would never be another football team in Crisfield. Don't you, people, know that you're allowing rules that were made over sixty years ago to still control you today? You don't see that you're allowing uneducated people to rule you, but that you are still being governed by dead people?

The Black boys are playing football in Fruitland, and they are the stars up there. Don't you understand that this could be happening in Crisfield if the Black and White boys were on teams together? The talent is here, but you, people, are so stuck in the olden days that you can't see the present as well as the future. Where's your vision? I guess that the White people have not heard that "Where there's no vision, the people perish!"

This is a true statement, and there is evidence there that the town is dying. The many people there have dwindled down to a few hundred. The old people have died off, and most of the younger people have had to leave as there are no jobs. Many people have seen the potential of a place like Crisfield, but the greed and lack of vision has caused the town to die. Other places are doing things to try to make their hometowns grow. The people that are in charge of Crisfield want to keep everything the way it's always been.

There are not enough students to keep the one high school open. The best thing for the county would be to build one central high school, and then it would be able to provide programs to accommodate all of the children. The school could be state of the art. Instead, the high school in Crisfield moved the head start program into the high school building. Now, when asked for the enrollment of the school, they can give a false amount of students. The head start program consists of children between the ages of three and five. No one asks the ages of the children in the building. All they care about is the number. These children are listed on the books as total students for the high school. The state doesn't come to the school to find out the number. If the school doesn't complain, the state is satisfied.

The people of the area don't realize that this is holding their children back as they are not receiving the new programs that they should be. That would have allowed them to stay up with the world outside the small, no-vision town. The people don't realize that life is moving on outside of Crisfield. The people there feel that everywhere is like it is at home. It is so sad that I am known as a troublemaker because I am trying to inform and educate the citizens of what is going on.

I realize that I am putting myself in danger as well as being cared for even less, but I love Crisfield and would like for the people to hear the truth, and maybe they will wake up. This is not for Black people only. This is for all the citizens of the lower Somerset County.

Segregation vs. Integration
Which Is Better?

Next week I will turn sixty-four years old. For this reason, I am old enough to have lived in the life of one who was born before this integration. I lived long enough before integration to have formed an opinion on results of integration.

I will say that I was alive when the great struggle was being fought for this life of integration. There were many lives lost, many heads banged on, and limbs maimed and broken. Many days and years of jail and prison time issued for this great word of integration.

I now ask the question, was it worth all this for this result? What is life about today that is so much better than life was before all the pain and agony that is present today? I would like to take a personal hard look at this question.

I was born on June 7, 1952, in the United States of America, a place of segregation. Is life better or worse today? I ask that you come and take a journey through time with me, and let's look at the history.

As I can look back in my life from when I was about two or three years old, I can remember sitting on my mother's lap as she read to me. I did not know what the feeling was then, but as time had gone by, I realized that I had a feeling of love and safety. I can remember being dressed and taken to a place and left there with an old lady and a lot of other people of my size for a long period of time. There was sometimes a lot of noise such as crying, and sometimes a lot of quiet as the children were asleep. I hope you realized that I am telling you is that I was at the babysitter's house. The greatest thing that I am telling you that I looked forward to everyday was seeing my mother came in and took me home. I did not know when, but it felt very good to wake up and not have to leave home and go to this place.

There was a time in my early life that my father was working only on piece work. We called it later in my life "hustlers." There were no full-time jobs for Black men in my hometown. The men that wanted to work had to find jobs to work daily. They would go to various places and asked owners of business if they had odd jobs for them to do for the day or by the week. They would take any job available to make money to feed their families.

In my family, there were six children and both parents. My mother picked crabs in the warm seasons. This was from say March through early October. The other months, she would draw unemployment from the state. The amount that she would get per week may have been about ten or fifteen dollars. My father would get jobs doing whatever. I was not school age so the many jobs that he went on, I was with him as they could not afford to pay the babysitter.

There were some jobs that he had to take that I could not go with him. Sometimes I went to the crab house with my mother. There were only Black women picking crabs. Sometimes there were a lot of children in the crab houses with their mothers as they could not afford to pay a babysitter.

We were not allowed in the crab houses legally as we were too young. Whenever the inspector came around, our mothers were warned, and they would take us out and hide us, not that they would not get fired for having us in the crab houses. When the inspector would leave, our mothers would take the claws from the crabs and give them to us. We would crack claws while our mothers were picking the crabs. During the day, I might crack about five or six cans. This was over a pound. It takes five cans to make a gallon. Our mothers would make seventy-five cents or a dollar for a gallon. The owners of the crab house would take the gallon to the city, and the people would pay them ten or twelve dollars per can. This means the owners of the crab houses would make fifty or sixty dollars for five cans but only paid the Black women one dollar for five cans. The owners would make forty-nine or fifty-nine dollars clear on the five cans. This was a legal way of stealing.

My father would have to do field work at times to make money. He told me that he picked strawberry to work to raise money and would be paid one penny for two quarts of strawberries. I worked along with my older brother in the field with my father to help make money for the family. My older sisters would go to the crab house with our mother to pick crabs to help make money for the family. Most families were large as the children had to work to feed the family alone with the parents. Let me say, we were poor, but we did not know it as all families were the same. In those days, families would help other families to survive.

Then the day came that I did not go to the babysitter any more. This was where I started to go to school. In my early days, there was no pre-k or kindergarten as it is today. Once in the 1st grade, I could remember learning to write, read, go to the bathroom alone. I learned to open a carton of milk. I was given a small red plastic thing to keep in my pocket. When I went to the gym, I would give this plastic to a lady and walk a little farther and pick up a tray, go to my seat, and eat the food on the tray.

The gym in my school was also the cafeteria. As I sat in my classroom at a certain time, I could hear children outside playing. My class could not go outside to play alone. Whenever my teacher felt like it, she would take us out and we played games together. The older children were able to run around and play as they wished. Everyday started with devotion. There would be a classmate standing in front of the class at this time. There would be scriptures, prayer, and singing songs, and this happened every day. After those things were over, we would start our day with classwork. We would do the work that was given to us by our teacher. There was no laughing, playing, or talking while we were doing our classwork.

As we moved up in grades, we were given more freedom on the playground. We could play as we wanted to. Later, we would hear a bell ring, and that meant the playtime was over and now it was time to line up and go back into the school to do more classwork. When I got into the 7th grade, I felt that I was a big boy. I now would go to classes alone for a period and then move on to the next class. Though we moved from class to class, we were still organized. We walked up and down the hallways in straight lines. There were monitors on the hallways down the middle of the hall, and we passed them along orderly and quietly. If we talked on the hall, we had to stay in at lunchtime as a consequence for not obeying the rules of the school.

There were consequences for not following the rules of bad behavior. For this, students did the right thing. At those times, the teacher as well as the principal could spank us with a paddle for misbehaving. When they would paddle us, they would call our parents, and we would be paddled again once we got home.

In junior and senior high, in the morning, before the bell rang, we could be in the hallways, stand and talk to friends in the classroom or even be outside. Once the bell rang, every class came to order. Everyone would sit down in their seat and be quiet. This would be time for devotions. At this time, lunch orders were taken. The teacher would take attendance and all news was given for the day and upcoming events of the school. This was settle down time to start the day.

On the streets, there were water fountains. There was one fountain that had a sign on it, WHITE ONLY, and the other fountain had COLORED ONLY on it. There were bathrooms side by side. One had White only and the other had colored only on it. As a child, I wondered why. When no one was around, I tried the White only water fountain. I found that the water was the same. I did not go into the White only restroom as I knew that someone may be there as I was coming out.

When I went to the movie theater, there was the same, there was an upstairs and a downstairs. The Blacks had to sit upstairs. Also, there was a dividing shelf separating the Blacks from the whites upstairs. The White children (teenagers) would throw bottles, cans, or other items over the rail downstairs. They would throw it to the side downstairs that was in front of the Black people's side. When someone got hit downstairs in the White section, the police would come upstairs and take a Black boy down and put them out of the movie theater for the incident. We were blamed though the officers knew that we did not do the crime. If the boy that was accused resisted, he was hit with the nightstick and taken to jail.

If we wanted food from the restaurant, we could not go inside. We had to go around outside to the back door to order our food. No matter if it was raining, snowing, wind blowing, or whatever, we had to stand outside until our food was ready. There was a swimming pool in the town. When we found out about the pool, we started to go to it to swim. We were not welcomed. When we got into the pool, the White parents would take their children out. I guess we had some type of disease. Well, we did not care that they got out, this was more room for us.

As you may know, the White parents did not like that, so they had to come up with a way to keep us away from the pool. They had meetings on what to do to keep us away. They came up with the idea to charge a dollar to swim. Yes, a dollar was a lot, but we came up with money by doing things for people in our community. We even picked up soda bottles and took them back to the stores as we would get a nickel for every bottle that we brought in. One dollar was not enough to keep us out. They raised the price to come in to two, three, and four dollars. Whatever the amount, we could come up with it. Just know, the White people did not have to pay at all. When we came up with the money each time, the price was raised, they had to find another way to keep us out.

Well, the pool was in the marina where boats were docked. During that time, Black people did not own boats. There were only about three families that had boats. If others had boats, they were not parked in the marina as they could not pay the fee that was necessary to house them there.

So we did not have boats. The next meeting introduced the idea that one could not swim or use the pool unless they have a boat in the marina. That was the way that we were kept out of the pool. Guess what, many of the Whites did not have boats either, but they were still allowed to swim without paying. The bay was nearby, so many children learned to swim outside in the bay. Things came hard for Blacks, but that did not stop us. When things were hard, it made us work harder to achieve the goal. I may only have one or two pairs of pants, but guess what? I took care of them.

We worked in the fields picking strawberries for ten cents a basket, twenty-five cents a basket for tomatoes, and thirty-five cents a basket (not sure what is here). We were taught that when life gets hard, don't to quit, just buckle down, work harder. Pick harder and faster and you can get ahead. There was once a commercial on the television that was done by a Black person. It stated, "All that I ask for is a chance." We knew that if we were given the opportunity to do the same thing that the White child was given, we would do the task and do it better. We knew that, and the White people knew it also. In the Black communities, it was said that it takes a whole village to raise a child. Children were taught to respect all elders. If the elders saw you do something wrong, they could correct us.

I remembered one day when I was in the 4th or 5th grade, water stood along the street beside the pavement. The boys would make stick boats to pull along in the water. A boat consisted of a board with a nail stuck to one end sticking up. Then we would tie a string to the nail and pull the boat along in the water. My boat got caught on something in the water as I was pulling, and my string broke. Well, I yelled out, "SHIT!" I did not know that a lady was walking behind me and heard me. She said, "What did you say?"

I did not answer as I know that she heard me. She took me by the hand, picked up my boat, and pulled me into the alley where we were and started to beat me. When she was finished, she put the stick down and told me that she was now going to take me to my mother. I said to myself, *Oh, you're going to get now. You beat me, my mother is going to get you.* I began to get happy on the inside because I knew that she was in trouble. Well guess what, I should have known that I was the one in trouble when we got to my house and the lady walked on inside without knocking on the door. She pulled me in and proceeded to walk through the house, calling for my mother. My mother was in the back part of the house into the kitchen. I heard my mother say, "I am in the kitchen. What you want?"

When the lady got me to my mother, she said, "I just beat Bernard down the street."

My mother said, "You did."

I am happy now as I know that this lady was going to get it. Well, my mother said, "What did he do?"

The lady said, "He hollered out SHIT!"

My mother said, "Thanks, you got him, and now I'm going to get him again."

My mother got her strip that she used on me and my brother and beat me again. An adult could do that in our community in those days. Whenever we were seen doing wrong, they could beat us or tell our parents, and the parents would beat us.

One day, me and two of my friends had gone off to play. We knew that we had to be home before the streetlights came on. For some reason this day though, we were not somewhere playing together, we all were still out after the streetlights came on. We lived real close together, so our mothers had a meeting in front of our houses to ask each other if they had seen us. Each said no. They then went into different directions to look for the three of us. As fate would have it, neither of the mothers found their own child. However, when they found us, each mother beat the boy that they had found, and there was no problem.

One day when I was in 6th grade, one of the girls in my class for some reason wanted to show off bad. She was bad this day beyond reasoning. The teacher told the principal, and the principal called the mother. The mother told the principal not to do anything to her. She was coming out to the school on her break at nine o'clock. The principal just let her go. Well, her mother came to the school and proceeded to our classroom. Our room was solid panel at the bottom but one could see-through the glass at the top. The girl was playing so much that she did not see her mother at the door watching her.

After a while, the mother opened the door and came into the room. She called her daughter to the front of the room. The mother took the yardstick off the ledge of the blackboard and proceeded to beat her daughter's legs. The girl was wearing a dress, so the mother had all legs. As the mother beat her daughter in front of the whole class, no student laughed at our classmate. Why not? We all knew that if we had laughed at our classmate, we would have been next. When we showed off or did wrong, there were consequences.

For the people that rode the bus to school and home, there were monitors on the bus as well. If we were too loud or playing on the bus, when we got to school the next day, there were consequences. When we returned to school, we were punished by the principal or stay in during recess. In the all-Black schools, we learned respect, manners, and other life skills. We were taught that when someone did something for you, you were to say thank you. When we saw adults talking, we stood and waited to be recognized. Once you were able to speak, we said excuse me then proceeded to say what we were interrupting for.

If you were handing someone something pointed, you took the pointed end in your hand and placed the item to them by the other end. We were taught manners and courtesy. We were taught to help when it was needed and not to laugh at anyone for the failures or shortcomings.

We were taught to use as much of our brain that we could. We were taught to reason things out and how to adjust, not just act, when faced with situations, as well as think things through before you speak or act when on the situation. We were taught that children were seen and not heard while in the company of adults until recognized by the adult to speak.

Our history teacher made a list of about one hundred and fifty to two hundred people in history that we had to look up in the encyclopedia to find out how they were important to society. Each of the people had to attest one page long about their accomplishment in society.

We as students complained and told our parents what we had to do. There was no need of doing. Our parents agreed with the teacher and made sure that we did all the work. The teacher told us what was to be included in the reports. If we did not have enough paper, we were to find paper bags, cut them open, and do the work on the bag. There was no excuse for not having the work done by the length of time given to complete the work.

As I stated before, we had to reason how to do the work. Groups of students got together to do the work. Each person from the groups were given several people to look up. When we had completed the number that we had, we would exchange the papers and copy the person down until we completed the task. When we first started, we all complained. Once our parents agreed with the teacher, we went on and did the work with no complaints. Now our pride took over, and everyone wanted to do the work and complete it before the other groups.

Our music teacher did the same with singers and composers. She had about one hundred and fifty to two hundred individuals that we had to do the same thing for. Our English teacher complied about twenty-five to thirty poems that we had to learn and recite within a certain length of time. The students of my day and before were always being challenged to do better. I was even challenged by my basketball coach when I was in the 10th grade. One day while walking down the hall before basketball practice, my coach stopped me along the way and said that I could do much better in my classes as well as on the court if I worked harder. He said that he challenged me for whatever. I asked him what that meant. He explained, and I became a better student as well as a better athlete. The teachers really cared about the students and their progress. We were often given brainteasers to solve to keep our minds sharp.

When adults spoke, children listened. When teachers or the school had rules, the parents went along with them, and the children had to obey. When we disobeyed the school rules or community rules, there were consequences that fit the situation. When we did wrong, our parents would not lie for us or that we could get out of the consequence.

When I was in high school, the Vietnam War was real hot. It was greatest for my understanding in my senior year in school. This was the first year of total integration over the country. There was no more White schools or colored schools. All children went to the same schools depending on the grade level.

Before this, the adults did not even work together. There were no Black people working in banks or the stores in my town, not in restaurants or even the fire departments. There was a Black section and a White section of the hospitals. If all the rooms in the Black section of the hospital were full, a patient was left on the hall until there was a space for them in a room.

My father worked at a crab house and helped unload boats when they would come to the dock to bring the crabs that were sold to the crab house owners. He said that one day while working on the dock, a little White boy was following him around as he worked. He became so annoyed that he stopped and asked the boy why he was following him so much. He said that the little boy told him that he was following him to see where his tail was hidden. He said that his father had told him that all niggers had tails and he was following to see where his tail was.

I told you earlier that Blacks were not allowed to go into White-owned restaurants. One day when I was in about the 6th grade, I had done enough to have money enough to go to the restaurant to buy some food. I had a taste for a cold cut sub. I took my money and went into the restaurant to order my food. I not only went inside but I sat down on a stool and proceeded to turn around and around on the stool that spins. I did not know what possessed me to do that, but I did. No one had ever told me to do it, I just did. Back in those days, Blacks were put out of White restaurants, and if we did not leave, the police were called and we were arrested. I heard that God takes care of babies and fools. Well, being in the 6th grade, I was not a baby.

Whenever we played sports and played against White boys, we always beat them. While growing up, I did not ever remember losing to a White boy or team doing anything.

Back in the sixties, White schools would not play against Black schools as they were not good enough. They could never beat the Black teams once we knew the sport. The one sport that they could beat us playing was soccer or crab soccer. This was because we did not have many sports in our schools. Once we learned how to play the sport, we would beat the White boys.

During the winter months in our community, neither the Black nor the White schools had football teams. We would always get together at the White high school and play tackle football without pads. For years we played Black against white football. We played every Sunday, but there was never a fight on the field or after the game by anyone. In all the years that we played, Sunday after Sunday, year after year, we never had a fight. These games took place when I was in my mid to late twenties. I only weighed about one hundred sixty pounds. I was very skinny but also very fast. Many times, I play defensive end on my team. The White team would put a boy at tackle that weighed over two hundred pounds to stop me. Sometimes they would double-team me with the tackle and tight end trying to stop me. They both could not stop me from getting to the quarterback. My team's front four had a saying, "Let's shake hands on the quarterback." The White boys' offensive line was too slow to stop us. They had no passing game as we did not give the quarterback time to see down the field to find his receivers. Our two backs were so fast that the receivers could not get open if he tried a quick pass. They had one big and powerful running back, but we had strong linebackers. Once the front four cleared out their offensive line, our line backers could stop their running backs before they could gain any yards.

For the four or five years that we played, they never beat us, not once. We had a softball league that the White boys played the Black teams in. There was one good White team, and they could win some games, but they could only beat the weaker teams. They could not beat the best Black team.

For years, the league was in place for about ten years. I don't think that either White team ever won a championship. When the league was going on, the Blacks and whites would put a team together and go to other leagues for tournaments or on the weekends and bring the trophy back to our town.

The various town fire companies would form tug-of-war teams to compete against other towns' fire stations. As I told you before, there were no Blacks in the fire companies. However, whenever the fire company in our town was going to compete against the company of another town or city, they would pick the strongest Black men of our town to go with them to compete. They always won the first-place trophy. They were so racist in our own town, but they would want the Blacks and would work together to win the trophy.

When our high school competed against the White high school, in our conference, our varsity coach would not let our varsity team play them. He always sent the junior varsity team to play their varsity team. We would beat them.

In the sixties, the White coaches said that Black boys were not smart enough to play sports with the White boys. I have never figured out why they would say that when anytime that they did compete against the Black teams, they would lose. The Black boys were more athletic, faster, and everything else. I never knew what it meant to lose to white boys at anything when we did compete against them.

When I was in high school, I never knew what it meant to have a new textbook. There were two high schools. Whenever the Board of Education decided that our end of the county need new books, they would give the new books to the White school and the Black school would get their old books. All the places in the front of the book where the names were to go were already filled as the White students had used them before it got to us.

Though this was true, we still had doctors, lawyers, dentists, teachers, preachers, CEOs, and business people to leave our school. We were taught to do the best that we can with what we had. We as students never looked at the books as drawbacks as we never knew any better. This was what we always had. The old books were still new to us.

Any equipment that we got came from the White school also. They always got the new equipment, and we got what they were through with using. When I was in school, we got our report cards every six weeks. That was a good term. Each school's honor and credit roll were put in the local newspaper. There were more students in the White school than in the Black. Therefore, their list of honor and credit rolls were longer than ours. Once the schools were integrated, we found out that the White schools, the people with the most affluent last names, were always either in the honor or credit rolls. This was true in high school, but when they graduated and went on to college, the most of them flunked out of school. We even found out that some of the students had nervous breakdowns once they got into college. Some had their parents attend classes with then as they could not keep up. Many did not go to college at all though they were supposed to have been so smart in high school. They were no smarter than us at our high school. They just got what they did because of who they were, the family that they were in.

All of America saw that when the Vietnam War was going on. Whenever some of the rich White boys were drafted in to the armed forces, if their parents had enough money, they would send their sons to Canada. If any Black boy was drafted and would not go, he could not afford to go to Canada, we went to jail. We even lost our civil rights and citizenship. After the White boys were in Canada for about six to eight months, they could come back home with amnesty. They retained full honors from this country. Nothing was lost. Some may not have stayed in Canada that long. They came back as soon as the heat was away from their name. Many probably never even went to Canada. They just had a Canadian address.

Please, stay on this journey through time with me. I was a junior in high school, and our teachers were beginning to inform us of what was going to happen next year. This was the '68–'69 school year. They were telling us that we will be going to school with the White students next school year. We were prepared to compete with those students. We did not go over to that school and not know how to behave. We were already being taught to always do our best at whatever we did, not to make excuses for failure and reason situations out before trying to solve problems. We were always given classwork that we had to dig into the article or situation to find the answer. As you know, these situations kept us sharp and thinking to complete any task.

There were no cell phones, calculators, or other technology to do our work. We had encyclopedias that we had to use to look up answers to the task at hand.

The area that I grew up in was the seafood capital of the world. If you want to know where I am from, then go to the archives of your history and find where the seafood capital of the world was, and you will know where I am.

Well, the jobs of the people from my hometown was mostly in seafood. Here was where most of the seafood was exported from for the whole country. The seafood house owners had a legal slavery going on in their packing houses. You ask, what do I mean by saying that? Well, let me explain. Most of the city counselors or officials owned the seafood packing houses. This was where the crabs were picked and other seafoods were prepared before they were shipped to various parts of the country. Most of the labor in these packing houses was done by women. They picked the crabs and put them into pound cans to be sold to the public over the country. It took five-pound cans to make a gallon.

Now, pay attention so that you can understand what I am saying. Follow me: each can is a pound, it takes five cans to make a gallon. The packing house owner paid the ladies one dollar per gallon picked. So if a lady picked ten gallons per day (this was not hard to do by many ladies as they were fast with their hands), they made ten dollars that day. Well, the owner made five hundred dollars that day for the ten gallons while each lady made ten dollars. Now let us look at a whole packing house of women picking per day. All may not have gotten ten gallons. Some may have picked more and some less, but you now can see the legal slave labor that was going on in the community per day.

All the city officials were packing house owners; therefore, they would not allow any other type of workforce or business to come to the city as they did not want the competition for their workforce. There were enough people to work at any type of jobs that were present, but as they had the control, they did not have to compete with no other type of workforce. The people in the area were mostly only high school graduates; therefore, they did not understand that life could be different. Many never left the area; therefore, they felt that life was the same everywhere.

Once I graduated from high school and left the area and went to college, I realized the slavery life that the people of my hometown were still living. I went away to college and attended Bowie State College to further my education. I was able to have a car while in college. Therefore, I was able to travel around and go to stores whenever I wanted. As I would go to grocery stores, I was able to see the crab cans and even oyster cans of seafood that had been packed in my hometown. As you know, the owners had their labels on the cans to advertise their product. When I saw the cans and prices that the companies were getting for the product, I was able to realize that the packers were cheating the workers. I later found out that the owners were bragging to each other and other White people that they could take the money made in one day and pay all their workers for the whole season. The other days in the summer, money made was profit. Remember how I explained the laborers were paid. Each packing house had twenty-five to thirty ladies working per day. Some had more.

When I went home, I tried to get the ladies to go on strike for more money. As you may know, I was labelled a troublemaker by the packing house owners. They told the workers not to listen to me as I was trying to start trouble. The owner had the ladies brainwashed as they made them feel that they were their friends. They were able to brainwash them as if the women need to borrow money; they could go to their boss to borrow money. What I was trying to tell them was "as much money that the packer is making on you, if you make them pay you more money per gallon, you will not have to borrow." I could not make them understand that if they went on strike, the owners had to pay what they asked. Other type of workforce could hire other people to their work if the workers went on strike, but the seafood owners could not go out to other places to find laborers to do their jobs. They would have to pay what the ladies asked or lose a lot of money. They could not let the seafood sit long or it would spoil from the heat. The ladies were much older than myself, and they had been doing this type of work for this price so long that they would not listen to me. One thing was for years before as I was growing up, they were not even getting a dollar per gallon. At some point in life, they were only getting fifty cents per gallon. Now, they were getting a dollar. They felt that I was a troublemaker and I could make the boss mad and he might put them back at fifty cents per gallon.

Many years later, say in the eighties, the owners started to pay the ladies ten dollars per gallon. That was still no money as they were now getting twenty-five dollars or more per pound. That gallon was now selling for one hundred and twenty-five dollars and more.

Today, all those seafood packers are dead, and now there is only one or two seafood packing houses left. Yes, the packers are dead, and they were millionaires, but now, most of their money is gone, and their descendants were not as well off. They are now living no better and some not as well as the Black families that were cheated so badly years ago.

We used to go into banks and other stores and see that only White people worked there. This made Black people feel that the White people were so more important or richer than we were. They had the nice cars and big homes. We looked at them as being so much better than us.

As we got older, we found that they had no more than we did. There were programs in place that we as Blacks did not know about as we were not in the job force that would let us find out. Let me show you a few things. If a Black man bought a home or car and we could not pay the payments, the White people were the car dealers and home loaners. We had to go to them to buy the product and then to them if for some reason we were short and could not make the payments.

The loan officers would take our cars, put out of our homes, and not care about us. The White people would have the same situation, but the loan officers would tell them that they could pay only the interest and keep their homes or cars. When times got hard for Black people, we would lose our whatever. When times were hard for Whites, they could get around the situation. Even after integration and now I am a schoolteacher, there were and even now "die hard" that want things as they were before integration. I am a schoolteacher and am paid on the fifteenth and thirtieth of every month. I would go to the same bank each pay period to get my check cashed. I had gone to this bank every pay period for two or three years to get my check cashed.

I had been waited on by this same lady many times. She knew me from waiting on me so much, but this Friday, the bank happened to be full of White people, and I was the only Black person in the bank. As I was in line waiting my turn, there were other people in line, and there were some standing around talking. There were two other tellers waiting on people as well. It just so happened that I was in this line. As I got to the window to be waited on, I gave my check to the lady as everyone else before me had done and as I had always done before when I came to the bank. I did not know what got into the lady this day, but I guess she just felt like getting nasty or just get on the nigger day. As I gave her my check, she took it and said, "Who are you?" She proceeded to ask the other tellers if they knew me. I do not know what they responded. I think they went on to wait on the people that they were working with.

The lady began to ask the other people in the bank if they knew who I was. I said to the lady, "Hold it." Everything in the bank stopped. I said, "You know who I am, I come in here all the time, and you have waited on me many times before. I do not care if no one else knows me, you do, so cash my check and do not ask anyone else again who I am. Don't you ever do this to me again when I come in this bank." I guess she got scared and looked around for some man to help her, but now, everyone was looking at her. As no one said anything, she went on and cashed my check, and I left. I do not know what was said after I was gone, but I did not care. There may have been some Blacks that would allow that to happen to them, but I was not the one, then or now.

I was always taught in school as well as at home to respect my elders. However, I was taught not to let anyone disrespect me either. I remembered my mother telling me that I was no better than anyone, but no one was any better than me. I remembered that one day I took my little brother to the store as my mother wanted something from the store. He was in about 5th or 6th grade. I had him to stand in line to get whatever it was that we had to get. I went to the front of the store to wait for him as the line was long. Now, he had gotten to the cashier to pay for his items. As he was about to have the cashier to check the items, a White man jumped in front of him and the other people behind him to get his items first. The man said that he was in a hurry and had to go. I was about seventeen, and I said, "I do not care. You may go in front of the people behind my brother, but you will not be going before him as he has been waiting for his turn as he was supposed to move."

The man looked at me, he looked at my little brother, and then he looked at the cashier. By this time, I was standing next to him moving his stuff so that the cashier can wait on my brother. He did not like it, but he moved. I was taught to not let anyone take my kindness for weakness. I always stand up for myself. I had never needed integration, I would have been satisfied with separate but equal.

There have always been laws in our country, but I am old enough to know that. If there are laws that the White man disagrees with, they can change them. Therefore, there are so many amendments to the constitution. Some are good for Blacks, but they are made because the White man received benefits from them.

Before the time of integration, there was respect on every level. Children respected their parents and all other adults. Children were respected by their parents and other adults if they were doing the right things. We even respected the drunks on the street. When they spoke, we listened. If we did not respect even that drunk on the street and they told our parent, we would still be in trouble. Children were seen and not heard unless given permission to speak. You may say this is wrong, well guess what, we respected adults in all things. Not in just we wanted. If we did not have respect for the drunks on the street, this would mean now that we could choose who to respect and who we did not have to respect. In my time growing up, the younger brother or sister I had to respect and obey the older brother or sister. Even something as petty as riding in a car. If the older sibling wanted to sit on the front seat, the younger sibling had to move to the back seat even if the younger was in the car first. If your older sibling was picked up from school or some other place and you were already in the car on the front seat, the younger sibling would get out and move to the back seat. No one had to tell us to move, it was a known. We just got up and moved unless the older sibling said that it was okay and they would get on the back seat.

While in school, what the teacher or principal said was gospel. There was no argument. We just did what was told to us by the adults. My father was a minister and a very wise man. He used to say to me when I first started teaching school, "If you never let the horses out of the stable, they will never run. But if you let them out into the open range, it will be hard to catch them." I found this to be true in my thirty-nine years of teaching school. I never played with my students. I never made them feel that we were on the same level. Since this was true, I never had problems with children that other teachers had. Each class that I had when school started would say that I was mean. After they were in my class for a while, I became their favorite teacher. They found that I was not mean, I just did not take any stuff from anyone.

Now, continue to journey with me after the thing integration has started. First, we had moved from our all-Black schools where there was safety, love, and kindness. The place where children were children and the adults in charge.

The year of 1969–1970 was the first year of total integration of society and schools. This was the beginning of the end! Life has never been the same. This country had gone downhill ever since. I told my father early in the school year of my senior year of high school how things were now at the integrated school. He said then that there will be many changes in the schools. There were going to be a lot of problems. Yes, Dr. King along with other civil rights leader went through a lot of pain and other negative things to get equal rights. As time had gone by, I, along with most Black people that were alive before this happened, would and do love our freedom. However, we wish that the civil rights people had fault for separate but equal. We loved having the equal rights, but putting the country together has destroyed the Black race. I think that if I travel on this side in direction of the school systems, I could show the plight of the whole nation. As I have stated, my senior year of high school started the end of our country as from when and the reason it was founded.

When we as the Blacks moved from our all-Black school, if you paid attention, you could see the deterioration of the country. The principal, for some reason, called me to the office to be the spokesman for the Black children of the school. Later I found out why. He knew my father, and they played sports together or rather against each other as they grew up. He knew me from my father, but he did not know that I was the only child in the house with my father, his brothers, and their parents. I could be around them as they talked politics and the way the country was going.

I was able to participate in their conversations when they were talking about racial situations. When I got to school, and the principal called me to the office, I stayed focused so that I could hear everything that he said and was able to respond intelligently. There were some changes that had to be made for the school to satisfy the changes. We had to agree the school mascot and school colors. He stated that the White people of the school wanted to keep the school mascot, and the Black students could decide the school colors. He wanted me to speak to all the students from grades nine to twelve about this matter and some things that the other schools were having fights about. He told me that he was going to call all the Black students to the cafeteria so that I could talk to them. He then stated that there will be no adults in the area so we could speak freely.

At the all-Black school that we were coming from, there was no room intercom system. At this school, there was, I guess they did not know that I was smart enough to understand that; no, they were not in the room with us, but they could turn the system on and hear everything that we said. As I was in the room before the other students got there, I wrote on a piece of paper, very large, "Be careful what you say, the intercom is on, and they are listening to us."

They were already being dishonest with us and thought we did not know. Had I not been around my father with all his wisdom along with his brothers, I would not have known how they operate when I was a child. Another time he called me to the office. It was time to elect the school president. Now, he wanted me to speak to the Black student body for us to nominate two people to run for the office. Again, after talking with my fathers and his brothers, I was able to handle this task. I told the students that we were not going to select two candidates. We would only have one so that our votes would not be split. There was one thing that I did not cover. When the election came up, I did not think about the fact that I should have selected someone or myself to be present to help count the votes.

The White students had selected two candidates. This means that their votes were split. We only had one running for the office. When the results were given, the one Black person had lost the election by ten votes. We had every Black student from grades nine to twelve to vote for the one Black person. The White students' votes were split. They got us there.

Now, I want you to travel with me to this time of integration. I am going to the education of schools mostly, and this will show the country of today. I can use this avenue as I spent eleven years of school in the all-Black school. Then I was in the White school for one year and then taught for thirty-nine years. I know that I am qualified to make the intelligent comparison. I am now old enough to look back in segregation as well as integration.

To start this part of the journey off, this was the year 1969–1970. It was my senior year in high school and the first year of total integration of the whole country. There may have been some areas of the country that the schools were already somewhat integrated. Even in my area, a few years earlier, maybe in 1967, students could choose to go to either school, the Black school or the White school. A few parents decided to send their children to the white schools, but for the most part, the Black parents stayed in the Black schools. Now it's my senior year.

As I stated, teachers as well as the principal could spank students. Well, you know that was the first law that was changed over the country. There will be no spanking of students in school. When that happens, that was the beginning of the problem to get us to where we are today. After the spanking was taken out of schools, prayer was removed.

Let me start with the first day of school on my senior year. When we walked into the White school, the atmosphere was different. We, as the Black children, felt a fright as we were moving to change and to the unknown. The school was very loud, and the children were running up and down the hallways. As I was looking for teachers, I got scared because the white teachers were dressed just like me. I could not tell the teachers from the students. I started looking for Black teachers as I knew who they were. When the bell rang, things got a little less frightening. We were all told to go to the gym and have a seat. We could then see the Black teachers, and things were more under control.

All the Black students were sitting down and quiet as we knew that was what the bell meant. The White kids were in the gym, but they were running around and still talking and throwing paper at each other. This was a problem for the Black students as well as the Black teachers. When the principal came in and started to talk, the Black students were quiet trying to hear what the principal was saying. It was very hard to hear as the White children were not paying him any attention. He would call a teacher that had 9th-grade homerooms. That teacher would stand in the floor, and the children in their class would line up behind them as their names were called. Then they would follow that teacher to their homeroom. As the children would leave the gym, they would look at the other children as if to say, "Save me, where are they taking me?" The Black kids were walking in line, but the White kids were running around and playing as they left the gym. The Black children were used to walking up and down the halls in straight lines and quietly. When my class was called, it was the last class as we were at the end of the alphabet. When my homeroom teacher was called, then the roll was called, and we got up and followed him. He was a White man, and guess what, he wore a suit and tie. However, as we walked down the hallway to our classroom, the White children were out of control. They were all over the hall and hollering into classrooms as we went by the doors. There was nothing said to them for the disruption as we went by.

Once we were in the classroom, when the bell rang to start the homeroom period, the Black students found a seat and sat down, waiting to start morning devotions as we had done back at the all-Black school. We started to wonder what was going on as we were waiting quietly, but the white kids were still walking and talking all over the room. Some were sitting on the window ledge, hollering out to people as they walked pass the school. It was September, and the windows were open as it was still warm outside. The white students never sat down or stopped talking during the whole time. If the teacher asked them anything, they had to talk over the noise that the students were making. The teacher asked one boy when was his birthday as he was updating our personal files. We were seniors, and the boy said, "I do not know, stop worrying me."

One of the White girls told the teacher the boy's birthdate as he really did not know. Ha, this boy was on the honor roll every marking period as he was from a rich family. There was never any organization or order in the classroom the whole time while waiting to move to our first-period class. As stated before, at the all-Black school, we had to sit down and had devotions to prepare for the day. When the bell rang to move to our first-period class, we had to stay seated and wait for the teacher to excuse us. Since the White students never sat down, when the bell rang, they just picked up their books and stormed out the door as they were in the classroom. We, the Black students, were sitting, waiting to be dismissed. The teacher asked why were we still sitting as the bell rang for us to go to our first-period class. We told him that we thought we had to wait to be excused. He said, "No, when the bell rings, you are dismissed to go to your next class."

We got up to leave in a single file as we had done years before, expecting to see monitors on the hall, and we walk in single file quietly down the hallway. The students were all over the hallway, loud and bumping into each other just as if walking up and down a mall. Everyone was on their own doing as they please. The Black students were standing along the side of the walls as for real, we were scared as we did not know what was going on. We did not know the hallways as we were new to the school. There was no one there to give us any direction, so we were just as horses let out of the pin in a new yard, not knowing what to do.

This may sound as if we were dumb or ignorant, but it was not. We were used to structure. We were used to doing things organized. Now, all structure and organization were all gone.

There were no directions, and we were free to do whatever. We would go from class to class, the teachers would start class, but the students never stopped talking in either class. There was no teacher that had control of their classroom. The students did as they pleased and even called the teachers by their first names. The only class where there was teaching going on and the students were quiet in the classrooms was where the Black teachers were teaching. I did not have any Black teachers as the only class that I needed was senior English. My schedule was filled with electives. My 12th grade English teacher was a White lady, and she was a drunk. She assigned a novel of our choice to read every marking period. The English that she taught was the same thing that we learned the year before. The novel that I had to read was the only new thing that I had all year. Then that was not new really. I say that because I never read either book. We had to read the novel in the six-week period, but I only remember getting up and giving one book report. The one that I did give was at the end of the first period.

I read the foreword of the book, about the first twenty pages of the book. Then the last maybe twenty pages of the book. When I got up to give my book report, the teacher said, "Very interesting." I had read that book over the years, but I never got the perspective from my reading. I did not have much of a clue to what the book was about, but I just stood there and talked at least fifteen minutes about what I had read. When I finished, the teacher said that it was a very good report, and I received an A. I do not know if I gave another book report for the whole year, but I know that I received a B from the English teacher for the whole year. I was an academic student and played on the basketball team, so I did not have to attend any classes. I just had to check in at the start of the class and then I could leave. You might say that this was bad; however, I was a young Black man given the opportunity to walk around the school and do nothing. What else was I going to do as I did not have anyone to make me do anything else.

As I stated earlier, I only needed to pass senior English. Maybe that was why teachers would let me leave my classes. It did not matter to me, I just left. I graduated with a B average for the year overall. It was time to elect the school student body colors and mascot. For some reason, the principal always called me to the office to be the spokesman for the Black students for the school. Other schools were having lots of fights due to the racial differences of the respective schools. To try to avoid these problems in our school, the principal would call me to the office to iron the problems out as they would arise in other schools in hopes of keeping the same situation from developing in our school.

In this new school, we had an hour for lunch. At our old school, we had half hour and had to eat quickly as the lunchroom was also the gym as well as auditorium. We had to eat and get out fast as it was needed for the next gym class. Now at the new school, we had a whole hour free to do as we will and go where we wanted. You know that this was new and overwhelming to the Black students. We did not know what to do with ourselves. One thing that we all did was walk to the drive-in restaurant that was some little ways from the school to eat lunch. This restaurant did not even want Blacks to come to the restaurant before integration. Now, they found that they were making so much money on this new Black population at lunchtime that they changed their policy. We as children did not realize what was happening. We were just so excited to have the freedom and now the ability to go to the restaurant to eat. The main thing was the freedom to leave school in the middle of the day. We spent so much money in that first year that the restaurant owner remodeled his restaurant. We had sock hops during lunchtime as we had so much time for ourselves.

I had a car; therefore, I could leave school and take girls and do some good as well as bad things. Life began to change for Black students this first year. Many of the changes, as I think back, were very bad though they seemed so good at the time. The greatest thing that this started to change was discipline. Our parents had to work and did not realize what this freedom was doing to their children. We as Black children started to do things White students do that we knew would not have been accepted if we were still in our school.

We saw that White students went to the beer stores at lunchtime getting beer and bringing it back to the school and drinking it in the parking lots at lunchtime. We heard the White students calling the teachers by their first name and even their nicknames right in school. We heard that White students talking back to the teachers in class and nothing would happen. When I would tell my father the things that were happening in the school, he would say, "This is bad and will be really in trouble later in life." I did not really understand, but now as I am much older and a retired teacher, I can clearly see what he meant back in 1960 and 1970. He said that there were going to be a lot of mixed babies born as the young White girls were going to realize the lies their parents have been telling them all their lives were not true. They had always told their children negative things about Black people, and now the children are going to be going to school from kindergarten through 12th grade. The children are going to be playing together and becoming friends with the Blacks. They were going to say, "My parents have been lying to me all this time." Now, by going to school together and playing together, they were going to start working together. Now, let us look at the country, there are so many mixed children.

I often talk to my wife and say, "Look at those White grandparents with those mixed children. Many of them are the one that had lied to their children back in my day growing up that did not like Black people. Now, look at them, they have these mixed children as grandchildren and must have them with them in these stores, restaurants, and even their homes and cannot do anything about it. Life have come right into their homes. Now, they must live the lie that they told years ago." Everything that he told me back in the day is now true.

As I was still in high school, there was a White boy for some reason wanting to be my friend. I did not know why, I guess it was because I was one of the better athletes in the school and in the 12th grade. Maybe he saw that I was a person that no one would mess with. He wanted me to be his protector as we know that White people were scared of Black people for real. I guess he felt that being with me would keep everyone from bothering him.

Well, one day at lunchtime, he and I were walking down the hallways of the school. We were on one end of the hall, and his girlfriend and some of her friends were meeting us from the other end of the hallway. Well, right in stride, he said to me, "That is my girlfriend and her friends coming toward us, when they get to us, I'm going to kick you in your ass and you do not do or say anything."

I stopped talking and walking and said, "What did you say?"

He said it again, and then he said, "I've got to show her and her friends that I am superior to you."

I said, "What, are you crazy? Boy, you may have to make her feel that you are superior, but I'm not the one that you're going to use to prove that to them. If you kick me, they're going to have to call the ambulance and then the police. I'm going to mess you up bad. Don't you ever think that you can kick me because it will not work."

I really think that he got upset, but guess what? I did not care. He may have felt that he could do that to someone Black, but I was not the one.

There were times that the Black boys and the White boys would fight on the streets over the weekend. There was one incident that took place one weekend, and now it was Monday. I was now in my POD class. For you who do not know what this mean, it was Problems of Democracy class. This was a history class where issues of today were talked about. The teacher was a White man, and he was from West Virginia. This was a known clan state. He was now in our town and a teacher. On this day, as always, we were having racial discussions. In this class, there were about twelve or eighteen White students. There were only nine Black students. I was the only Black boy. We were always trying to find way to one up the other race.

This one girl stated, "I want to ask a question. Saturday night, my boyfriend was over to my house. When he left and was walking home, why did a group of Black boys stop him and beat him up?"

All the White students as well as the teacher said, "What can you all say about that?"

They were now looking at the Blacks in the class as they felt that they had stunted us. The Black girls were looking at me for an answer. The White students and the teacher were all cheering as we couldn't give an answer. Then I said, "I will answer that. How do you know that your boyfriend was so innocent?"

She said, "Because he had been over to my house all day. He could not have done anything."

I said, "He was over your house all that day, but where was he last week?"

The teacher said, "What does that have to do with what they just did to him?"

Then I said, "It's just like the clan. When they come to a Black man to beat him up or hang him, they put on their White sheets to cover their heads and bodies to hide. They come nine or ten to injure one Black man as they know that they could not do what they wanted to do to the Black man alone. When they are beating the Black person up, all that the Black man could see was their shoes.

No matter how bad the Black man was beaten, if he lived, he would remember the shoes of the clansmen. This is true of the Black boys that beat your boyfriend as he left your house. He may have been to your house at this time, but what about last week when those White boys, eight or nine, ganged that Black boy. It was dark when it happened, and all that the Black boy could see was the shoes of the boys that were beating him. There was one of the Black boys in the crowd that were beating your boyfriend at that time. Well guess what? They were not beating your boyfriend, they were beating the shoes that had jumped him before."

All the White students as well as the West Virginia teacher got mad. The teacher jumped across the desk and said, "That is enough discussion about this topic."

They turned red but could not say anything. I did not care, I was not worried about them doing anything to me or the other girls! The teacher said, "Class, over, let's go."

Now the Black girls were cheering as there was nothing that they could say.

As we move on, I told you that before integration, the teachers as well as the principal could spank or beat us if we did anything wrong. Well now that integration has started, the White people took spanking out of school. This was because the White parents did not want the Black teacher spanking their children. At that time, nothing happened to the White children if they did wrong in school as well as at home. "It took a village to raise one Black child, but the White children did what they wanted in school and at home." There were no consequences for bad behavior in the White communities in many homes. The parents may put the child in (time out) for a while. Time out usually was for a few minutes in their rooms. How was that punishment when the child had everything in their rooms? In the Black community, a child was beaten on their rear end for their misbehavior. This meant, "Don't participate again in the activity that got you that beating." As the Black children saw the White students get away with bad behavior and there were no consequences, they started to do what they saw the White students get away with.

As parents got younger, they started to let their children do the same thing. The beginning of the end. There was a law passed later that no parent could spank their child. If they did, they would be put in jail. I can remember when I was a child, I went to the grocery store with my mother. As we were walking the aisles, I saw some candy on a shelf. I reached down, took some, and put in my pocket. My mother saw me. I was about four or five. She took the candy out of my pocket, put it back on the shelf, and spanked my fingers. She said, "You do not touch anything that do not belong to you." Guess what, I never took anything that was not mine unto this day of writing this book.

As I am the seventh child of eleven, we were taught not to bother anything that did not belong to us. I can remember, that as a child, my mother or father put some money on the dining room table and left it there. I guess that it was about three or four dollars. We did not know then, but this was a test for all of us. Our parents later told us that they were trying us to see if anyone took the money. Well, none of us did. No, I'm not saying that we were perfect, but all of us passed that test. The one time that I did take something that was not mine was when I was in the 10th grade. It was basketball season, and there was a sweater that I wanted from the store to wear to the game very bad. I had maybe five dollars. The sweater was seven dollars and fifty cents. It was very pretty to me, and I had to have it. I walked around the store and found an item that was three dollars and fifty cents. I took the tag off the item that was three dollars and fifty cents and put it on the sweater. I threw the seven dollars and fifty cents tag away. I took the sweater to the cashier and paid for it. I left that store with my sweater, but I was scared for the next six months. I do not know if you have ever heard this saying or not, but it states, "Scared people cannot steal. They will get themselves caught." Well, I did not get caught, but I never stole anything again.

Now, as I got older, I saw White children taking things from the shelf, and their parents would see them do it. Some parents would try to make them put the candy back. However, if the child started to cry or tell the parent that they were not going to put it back, the parent would say okay and just pay for the candy. What was that teaching the child? This meant that whatever they did was okay. They knew that they would not get into trouble as their parents would fix it up for them.

Well, there were Black children that may have gotten away with stealing also. However, these were the Black children that found themselves in jail. They were getting by, but they did not get away. In time, they would get caught. In Black communities, there were consequences for misbehavior. The White children got away with their misbehavior. There were times that the White parent knew that their child was wrong, but they would go along with their child. They could pay to keep them out of jail, or they knew someone in high places to speak for them so their child could go free. The Black child knew this and tried the same, but they would end up in jail.

As spanking was taken out of schools and society, life started to change all over. The Black children started to do as the White children in schools. The problem was as the Black child would be punished for the same behavior and the White child got away with, the Black child started to rebel when they felt mistreated. This made the Black child angry, and then they would do even more. The White teachers were afraid of the Black children, and when the Black children would do wrong, they would just send them out of their classroom to the office. The Black child would be suspended. The White child would be sent back to class after a few minutes. The Black child was sent home. If they could not go home as there was no one to pick them up, they were told that they could not come back to school for the next three to five days.

We watched all things happen in that first year of full integration. Things went downhill as time went on. At my all-Black school, we did not have a variety of school sports. We only had basketball and track. Well, we excelled at both. Now we went to the White school. They had all types of high school sports. We did not even have good playground equipment. The only equipment that we had was what the Board of Education would give us after the White schools had finished with it. When they would get new equipment, they would give the old equipment to us. We were happy to get anything, as it was new to us. From all this, the student was taught to take care of whatever we had. We were taught not to complain but do the best that we could with what we had. We were taught this in school as well as at home. At home, we had to wear hand-me-down clothes and shoes. We had to appreciate those things, so we knew how to take care of the equipment in school. We were not allowed to make excuses for not having new materials. We were taught that this was what we had, so we had to do the best that we could with what we had. From all of this, we still had trophies in the trophy case from basketball and track. We had trophies from our singing choir, and the choir was known as the glee club.

From this came doctors, lawyers, dentists, teachers, preachers, high-ranking military officers, and CEOs. We did not get the best and new book for class or equipment, but we had those old, good Black teachers that were certified and brought the best out of us. We learned to accomplish much with very little. We were taught to wait our turn in life. Everything did not come at the same time. If you wait your turn and earn the "whatever," you will appreciate it more.

At the Black school, if a young lady got pregnant while in school, once she started to show, she had to drop out of school and could not come back until the next school year. Once we got to the White school, a girl could go to school until it was time to have her child. This was because those White parents were not going to make their daughters have to leave their friends and not graduate with them.

When the White girls would get pregnant, the parents would send them to another city where they had relatives. The girl would stay there until she had the baby. The child would be put up for adoption, and the girl would return to school as if nothing happened. The Black students did not know this until we went to school with them, and the other White students would tell us why the girl was not in school then they would have showed up months later. Some of the White girls had gotten pregnant by the Black boys. When the White girls would come back, they could tell the Black students that they were still virgins, they had gone on vacation. Once the other White students told us what had happened, they could not lie to us anymore.

Well, now it was basketball season. Soccer was over for the boys, and field hockey was over for the girls. As I told you earlier, we did not have many sports at the all-Black school. There was no soccer, so we were very good basketball players. When we got to the White school, our first unit in physical education was football. Well, the Blacks would always beat the White boys in class as we were faster and stronger. The next unit was soccer. Well, the Black boys knew nothing about soccer as we had never played before.

There was a good Black boy in the 11th grade for playing basketball. We were told that when his class started to play the soccer unit, the teacher did not teach the fundamentals. As the White boys already knew how to play, he just picked teams and told the boys to go and play the game. This good basketball player had possession of the soccer ball. The PE teacher yelled out "Dribble the ball" while running down the field. The young man heard the teacher yell out "Dribble the ball." The basketball player proceeded to pick the ball up and started to dribble the ball like a basketball game. Yes, you may get a laugh from this, but it was not the young man's fault as he did what he knew. The teacher did not do what he was supposed to do as he was to teach the skills of the sport and even do drills so that everyone would know how to play. He was to even do lead-up game before putting the soccer ball out for the students to play. I know that the teacher did not teach the skills for that class as he did not teach the skills to my class.

As did the other school in the area, we would have a JV and varsity teams for the school. There were at least forty to fifty boys to go out to fill thirty positions. In those days, the White coaches did not feel that Black boys were smart enough to play football and basketball with the White boys. You may not be old enough to know this, but we were not allowed to even go to the big White school for any reason until about 1965. The big White schools would not play the Black high schools or colleges before about '65. The Blacks were lacking in intelligence to be able to think high enough to perform on their field or in their gyms. If you have not heard of it, look on your computers to find old movies and find the movie *Glory Road* and watch it.

The White principal of my school told our coach that he could not have an all-Black basketball team. From 1965 until now, there are more and more Black boys on the various levels playing basketball. The coaches are realizing that if they wants to compete and win, they will have to play the Black boys. The principal told the coach that he had to have twelve boys on the team. He had to have six Black boys and six White boys. He also told the cheerleader coach that she had to do the same with the cheerleaders. Now, this was not stated for the soccer and field hockey teams.

As I stated, on November 15, there were forty to fifty Black boys to go out to play basketball when there were only thirty positions. Well, now there were no thirty positions as the principal have told the varsity coach that he could have only twelve players on his team. I think that the JV coach was able to have fifteen players on his team. From this tryout day, only two White boys went out for the varsity team as they knew that they were not going to be able to beat the Black boy out for the positions on the varsity team.

Do You Love Me or Are You Just Using Me?

I have been on this earth for sixty-five years. I was a child, an adult, a husband, a father, a teacher, and also a preacher. From these avenues, I have seen and learned many things. Some good, some bad, but all informative. Many lessons have been learned, and also I have taught many lessons

My life has been great; however, if I were not attentive as well as focused, things could have been very different. I am asking you to now go on a life's journey with me. The basic journey that I would like for you to travel with me in is in the world of sports. I have played many different sports. Also, in my life, I have coached many as well. I feel that I am an expert in the knowledge of sports.

In my years as a child, I lived in the world of segregation. I found out at an early age that I played sports very well. If you would allow me to say so, I was a very good athlete. I was and still am a great competitor.

I have never liked to lose and have never wanted to be on a team that was satisfied with just competing. If my teammates did not have a winning attitude or they were just satisfied with playing the game, I did not wish to play with them. When the game was tight, I never wanted to hear my teammates say, "We can't win." I have always felt that the game is not over until the final whistle blow or someone say it's over.

As my children became of age to compete, I instilled in them, "You never quit. You never give up. You never play unless you're willing to do your best. You always play to win." I let them know that you don't even let up because you're playing your girlfriend or wife. You may not play as hard when you know that you can beat your opponent at any time. I then said, "You may catch a cramp or get sick and that person or team may come back and beat you."

The bottom line in the game was, who won? No one cared whether you were playing easy or not. Everyone just cared about the wins or loses. Once you lose, you can't take that back. No matter what, that person could always say, "I beat you." I don't care how well you may be or how poor that person may play, they could always say, "I beat you." Therefore, always do your best.

I have an older sister that had a motto, "Any job big or small, do it well or not at all!" I learned that at an early age. If you are going to dig ditches for your job, be the best ditch digger. Always strive to do your best. I don't know about you, but a loss hurts me.

As I played and coached, I always have said, "When the game is over and you have lost, can you ask yourself or can you look into the mirror and honestly say to yourself I did my best? I left everything on the field or on the court." I realize no one can win all of the time, but can you honestly say that you lost not for my effort but the opponent was just better at this time? I have always said, "You might get me this time, but I will be back."

I sing in a church group of men. I am the president. We practice every week whether we have to go to a place to sing or not. Hey, the more you practice, the better you get. With much practice, and you're in a group or on a team, when one messes up, the others can pick you up. Many times you may mess up, but no one watching can tell as the other teammates will cover up the mistake and then you can get back on the right track.

When I was growing up, I played a lot of sports with fellows that were older than me. Sometimes that may have hurt, but it was for the best in the long run. I learned this at the age of about seven or eight years. I stayed with my grandparents. My grandfather was a checkers player. He would always want to play checkers with me. When I was that age and even when I got a little older, we did not have a television in our home. Since this was true, there were a lot of night that went by that we had nothing to do but sit around and listen to the radio. My grandfather taught me to play checkers at that time. I had a lot of hard lessons sitting across from him while learning this game. When he taught me the game, it was "straight pool." This meant that if you touched one of your checkers, you had to move it. As I was learning, there were a lot of times that I touched a man. He would say, "Take it somewhere, you touched it." That move sometimes caused me two or three men on his next move.

I can hear him now saying, if you don't know what you're doing, you better ask somebody! I would sometimes cry as he would beat me so bad playing. My grandmother would be sitting and reading the newspaper or doing whatever and would hear us playing, my grandfather teasing me, and hear me crying. She would say, "That's all right, Bernard, you just keep on playing, pal, you'll beat him after while." I don't know if that helped me at all as all I knew was that I was crying and he was laughing. To my surprise, after about six months, things started to happen. I found myself getting better and better!

I found myself winning some games. I found myself stop crying, and now I could talk. As time went on, I found that I was winning more than I was losing. Later, I found myself winning every game. There were times that my father and uncles were at the house when we were playing. I am beating my grandfather so much that one of my uncles would say, "Cha pal, get up, let me have him." After a while, I would beat that uncle. Then one of my father's other brothers would tell that uncle to get up so he could challenge me. This uncle was very good as I was good now. I never beat him in all the games that we played. Then my father would say to me, "Get up, Bern, I'll take care of him." Now my father and his brother would sit down and battle. All these things taught me to be competitive, always do my best, never give up and have a winning attitude.

Now as I was older and wanted to play with the older boys, I had to always work hard to play. It was known that if you could not play, you could not get on the "big court." All the best players were on this court. If you were not good enough, you had to play on one of the other courts. You played here trying to learn so that you could play on the "big court."

After a while, I was able to play on the big court with the older boys. I have a brother that is two years older than me. He would beat up on me playing sports. I didn't realize it then, but he was preparing me for the big court. I used to complain to my parents and grandparents, but I got no satisfaction from them. They would not say anything to my big brother. I didn't understand why they didn't. Years later, I found out why they didn't say anything.

When I was in the 8th grade, I was able to make it to the junior high team. I was the starting point guard. As time passed, I played all five positions. Even though I was only five foot three or so, I had good ball handling skills. I was a good jumper and could get rebounds. I was pawning the men's basketball when I was in the 7th grade. Our team was very good, and we won most of our games that year. When I was a freshman, I was on the JV and did not see a whole lot of playing time. There were also juniors and 10th graders on the team that could not make the varsity team.

We were still in the era of segregation, but we were now competing with the White schools in sports. In my area, the Black schools started to compete with the White schools in 1965. We were still in segregated schools, but the schools started to play each other in sports. When we played the White school, we usually beat them. In those days, University of Maryland College Park would not play Maryland State College (which is now UMES). Maryland State College always had good basketball teams, football teams, track teams, and baseball teams. Each sport had players to go on to the professional sport of their games.

For the Super Bowl that had the Baltimore Colts play the New York Jets, Maryland State College was the first college to have three players on each team. At one point, there were more players in the NFL from Maryland State College at one time than from any other school.

Black players of any sport were not allowed to attend any White college for any reason! We definitely could not attend the White colleges for sports. In football, we were not smart enough to play quarterback. We were unable to make decisions. These were the things that White people labeled us with.

As the years went by, Jackie Robinson became the first Black in professional baseball. Once he was able to show his ability in baseball, the door was opened for others in all sports for all Black players. This was a change that opened many eyes but was still not accepted by the White man. He still resisted the truth.

In our communities, we started to play sports against or on the same teams as the Whites. We had fun and competitive games, but that's as far as it went. The Black players were not able to think well enough to play on the same basketball team with the White players. If you ever saw the movie *Glory Road*, you heard the man say, "You don't play the Black players as you do the White." There was an unwritten rule for the amount of Black players that were on the court at a time at home and the number you put on the court at a time on the road.

As Black athletes, we could not compete with the White boys. Then some White coaches began to accept the fact that we need the Black players to win! They started to recruit one player to put on their team. I guess they began to realize that on the sandlots, they played with or against the Black players; "I need them on team that I am coaching now." They then found that player that they wanted and put him on his team. He found that his team was much better and started to win more games.

In the '60s, there was a commercial that come on the television, radio, and in newspapers that stated, "All I want is a chance." This came as the results of the Black person being given the opportunity to perform a task on the same level and amount of time as the White person at his skill level. The Black person performed the task as well or better than the White person. This was factual information. Whatever the job given to the Black person, the company improved its production. This was in any job, not just sports. I will attribute this performance ability to the background that the Black child hid from their school days.

The expectations that were put on the Black child in school from the 1st grade to the 12th grade was higher than the White children of the same age. In the Black schools, there were consequences for bad behavior. There were consequences for not doing your schoolwork as well as homework. I can remember hearing while in school, "You must work hard as a student because life is hard once you're in the world as an adult. No one is going to give you anything."

For this reason, as we grew up, we always worked hard and would do our best because we were taught that life is hard. This lesson carried over to life in sports as well as in the workforce once we were grown. I saw so many examples while growing up not to believe what my teachers and parents were saying to me.

The Vietnam War was in the late '60s and early '70s. There was a draft at that time for men to go to war. When your number came up, you had to go. The year 1969–70 was my senior year in high school. This was the first year of total integration of all schools. Since this was true, I went to an all-Black school for eleven years. I only attended high school with Whites for one year.

As I have stated before, I played sports and played well. However, coming from my all-Black school, we were unable to afford many different sports. At the all-Black school, we only had men and women basketball. We have a few track people that were very good. There were some people from my school that held records in track and basketball for years to come.

Now was the 1969–70 school year. As I stated, this was my senior year in high school. At this high school, we moved to the White school. They had more sports to offer than we had at the Black school. The facilities were better as the Board of Education gave all the books and equipment to them and not to us in the Black school. The new books and equipment always went to the White school. When they received the new things, we got what they were throwing away. When we got our books for classes, we were already seven to ten years behind the White students. Still, we had doctors, lawyers, CEOs, preachers, and teachers to come from our school.

This was true because we had teacher that cared about us and our future. Now, it was basketball season for the schools in my area. The season started on November 15. We were now about to try out for the basketball team for the school. There will be a varsity and a junior varsity team. Most teams had twelve to fifteen players. There were about forty-five young men that tried out for the teams. There were only two White boys that were trying out. These will be all new teams as we had new coaches. The two White boys were seniors; therefore, they were trying out for the varsity team.

The basketball coach was told that he had to have six Black players and six White players on the varsity team. How was this possible when only two White boys went out for the team? The coach was only in his second year at the school, and he was White. The coach informed the principal that he only had two White boys to come out for the team. What was his plan of action? The principal told him that he was to go to the soccer coach and ask him the names of his four best athletes. Then the basketball coach was to put them on the basketball team. As I stated before, the White people over the country had made up an unwritten rule as to how to use the Black players. In my school, the principal told the coach that he could only have three Black players on the floor at any given time. There was nothing said about how many White players that he could put on the floor at a time.

We went on and had a good season. My team went on to play for the state championship for our division. The games were played at 3:00 p.m. on Friday, and the championship was played on Saturday. The team that we played on Friday had only one Black boy. The White boys on our team were not basketball players. They were scared. Playing the way that we were, we were able to make it to the championship games.

Most of the teams that the other teams had played during the regular season were White only. Therefore that team was there to play us. Now they had to face us. Our team could not get the rhythm that we had all the regular season as these boys were fundamentally sound. If we had been able to play all five Black players, things would have been different.

That team built up an over thirty point lead on us. Now going into the last quarter, the fans in the stands started to chant to the coach, "Put five Black players in." The coach decided to do that. In eight minutes, we brought down the over thirty points lead to nine. We lost the game by nine points. If we had been able to play all five Blacks in the beginning, we would have blown them out. The coach had us sitting in a 2.1.2 zone. We went in the fourth quarter and pressed them and played man to man. If we had played that way before, the game would not have been close.

As time had gone by, the coaches have started to realize that if they want to win, they had better put the Black players on their team. The next thing that happened, the big White schools found out the real deal. Having these Black players on their teams, they were winning. Now, with the winning, their schools were making considerably more money. This changed everything. When money was involved, the White man will do whatever to get more. The colleges started to recruit the best Black players. They started to cheat in any way to have them on their team. They would give the players' family homes, cars, jobs, and whatever to get the best players at their schools. For this I am asking the question, "Do you love me, or are you just using me?"

The White coaches who had that unwritten rule have changed due to the money or they had died out. They will now do anything to have Black players on their teams. That trend went on for years. It ended up where the whole teams were becoming Black.

Some schools were "die hards" and would not use the Black players. If this was true, they only played the other schools that only had White players on their teams. When they only play White teams, they were still winning. When the time came that the NCAA started to make the schedules for the schools, they had to play the schools that had Black players in the playoffs. There was one team that stayed White and played the all-White schedules. They then went through.

As time had gone on, most sport teams from high school through the professionals started to be all Black. Then all the fans were excited for their team to win. There was no room in the teams for any White players as they were not as gifted as the Black athletes. The White athletes became managers and statisticians for the various sports. The gyms were full of fans as they were loyal to their home team. During this era, for some basketball teams in high school as well as college, the White coaches had an unwritten rule. One stated that you keep three White boys on the floor away and you play three Black players at home. There was no rule for the other sports as such.

However, it was a given rule that Black players could not play quarterback in football as we were not smart enough. We were not able to keep the plays in our head long enough to execute the plays.

Really, they didn't want us to play the offensive line, as they said that the plays were too complicated for the Black players. We were great on defense as we didn't have to think. We now only had to run over people and stop the ball. This would be easy as that required no thinking. This way of sports was great for a number of years. However, there were some die-hard coaches that refused to play Black players for any of their sports. They kept their teams all White and would only play other teams that were all White.

When things began to change, the all-White teams were forced to compete with the integrated teams. They would stay in their all-White conferences for the regular season. When it was time for play-offs and tournaments, they had to play the integrated and all-Black teams. Although they had done well in the all-White conferences, they now had to compete with the Black players.

There was one White player that ended up playing line for the Oakland Raiders that stated, "I am bigger and smarter, but I can't compete with the Black players in football. I lift a lot of weights and am strong, but the Black players still push me around. I've got to do something else to be able to compete."

In the '70s after I had graduated from college and was now a physical education teacher, every Sunday during football season, many men both Black and White would go to the high school in our town to play sandlot football. There were no pads, mouth guards, or anything used to protect us. We just played!

My friend and I would sometimes go to the college in our area to watch the college team play football against other colleges on Saturdays. When we would do inside to use the bathroom, the locker room was next door to the restroom. The door would be unlocked to the locker room, and we would go inside. We would find stray football cleats laying around. We would take one and move around the locker room to find another of the same size. We would match them up and use them on Sundays to play in against the White boys.

Oh, I guess I had better let you know, when we played on Sunday, it was after church. We always played the Black men against the White men. I wasn't as big as the White boys that they put on their offensive line as I played defensive end, but I was very fast. I was able to get past the offensive line and to the quarterback or running back. Before they could get past the line off scrimmage, I had already stopped the play. The White quarterback would have two of his men in front of me as to try to stop me, but I was too quick. The two men could not stop me. I kept the White team fussing as they could not complete any plays. Now as I was being double-teamed, that would leave someone else on my team open. This was still a problem for the White boys.

As the '70s went on, the White players could not stop the Black players, so they had to come up with something that would cause them to compete. This was when the age of steroids started. This made the White players bigger, stronger, and faster. For this, they now could compete better. They could not feel any pain. They then could compete as a person out of their mind. This made them great players, but there was a problem. Once they stopped playing, they would lose all the weight and strength that they had built up. The players even started to die as a result of not taking the drug any longer.

In baseball, the White players started to use steroids, and that started the era of the home run. Players started to hit seventy or more home runs per season. The sports officials knew about the players taking the drug but said nothing. Fans started to come to the baseball games, not for the game but for the home runs that were hit.

The interest of the fans was going down in baseball, and the sport needed something to get the fans back. The home runs were the answer. No one thought about the steroids, the arenas began to refill, and that was all that mattered. The problem came when the Black players started to use the steroids. Again, this made the Black player bigger, stronger, and still faster than the White boys. Steroids then started to be banned from the sports; all sports on every level. The athletics were now being punished for doing now what the professional league owners were using to get rich!

As teams on every level were able to compete and win championships, home team fans were very happy and excited.

As the years of 2000s came in, there have been another change in the sports arena. Before this time, all level of sports would do whatever to have the best Black players in their teams. The coaches, owners, fans would cheat to get the best players. They would give players money, home, jobs, cars, or whatever to have these players. They would move whole families to different districts in cities just to have these players playing for them. They knew that if they had certain players on their team, they had a much better opportunity to win the championship. Colleges and universities would give players good grades just to keep them eligible to play. The players didn't even have to go to class. They only had to enroll in the class, never attend, and they received an A for the course.

I was the assistant coach of a high school team in the '90s. We had a very good team; however, the player that was the best was not as smart as the rest of the team members. He was a nice kid, and he was not selfish on the court. He could have easily averaged twenty-five or thirty points per game. He was 6'4" inches tall and one of the tallest players in the team. This young man could play any position in the team. Because he was not selfish, he averaged about seventeen to eighteen points per game. This was great as there were other players that could score, so they were happy and that kept problems down. He was not asked to do this, it was just his personality. In his senior year of high school, we only lost one game. We beat every team that we played by at least twenty points the whole season. The loss was our first game of the season.

As stated before, this young man wasn't as smart as the rest of the team. This didn't matter; however, I asked to see his report card at one time. He had a 4.0 grade point average. I was shocked and then hurt when I looked at his report card. Oh, let me tell you, the principal of the school was also the coach of the football team and the baseball team. To let you know this man, I will tell you that he had the elementary school to hold his son in the 1st grade for two years as he had coached a long time and found that the White boys were at least a year behind the Black boys in developing as athletes.

The principal put this young man in the classes that he knew would keep him eligible to play sports. At the school, they had four-period block schedule. So this was the schedule for the Black young man in question. For his first-period class, he went to the middle school each day and directed traffic for the students and buses. For the second period, he was a tutor for the students. Remember, I told you earlier that he was slow. How could you tutor anyone? For the third period, he would come back to the high school, and this was his period of study hall. For the fourth period, he had weight training with one of the assistant coaches.

This young man's father was not in his life, and his mother was a crackhead living on the streets for the most part of his life. He had a sister who was only a couple of years older than he that was doing her best to raise him.

We were state champions in football and basketball during his junior and senior year of high school. In his junior year, the principal's son was the quarterback on the football team. The two of them set state records in throwing and receiving yards. The records held up for many years in the state.

The young Black boy told the coach and his son, "Whenever you are throwing the ball to me, you just get it in my area, I will take care of the rest," and he did. The school also won the state championship in baseball as the coach's son was a pitcher and shortstop. When he was not doing one, he was doing the other!

The Black young man graduated from high school and was recruited very highly by colleges. Once he decided which scholarship that he was going to take, the school had to test him. Remember, I told you that he was slow. Well, as a first grader, he was put into the special education classes as he was bad. He was never tested to be placed in these classes, this was just the way to keep him from disrupting the other classes.

His mother was a drug addict. She did not question the decision as she would receive a check for him from the state. She was happy to get the money at her son's expense. When the college tested him, he was found to be dyslexic. He had a problem from childhood that could have been corrected from the 1st grade with a pair of eyeglasses. He exhibited disruptive behaviors because he could not see!

The college that he chose told him that he did not have any credits that would allow him to enroll in their school. The White boy went on to college and played baseball and was even drafted by a professional baseball team. He did not stay with the team as he would have to be in the minor league for a few years. The young Black boy could not stay at the college that had recruited him. He was then contacted by a junior college in Florida. They sent him two tickets to come down to visit the school and find out if he would fit in.

I did not teach at the high school. Although I coached football and basketball there, I was thee physical education teacher at one of the elementary schools in the district. I was unaware of the young man's situation as it was going on. I found out later that neither of the coaches at the high school would even go on the trip to Florida with the young man. It ended up that his sister who was only a couple of years older had to go with him. If I had known before, I would have gone with him.

You may ask, why was this unimportant? It further gives me reason to ask, do you love me, or are you just using me?

After these two seasons, the principal left the high school and went on to the college level to coach baseball as the head coach, and he was the offensive coach with success in football. When his son graduated from college, he hired him as his assistant with the offense on the college level. With all this being said, the coach was a very good coach on the high school level as well as on the college level. He had much success at both. I must tell you, I learned a lot about coaching as well as being a leader of men from him.

As I was saying, as the 2000 years have started, the trend in sports was changing. There was another unspoken rule by the White people over the country. As one may listen or be in the company of the White parents, you can hear the displeasure in having the Black players on their teams. In my former high school before the 2000s, the White parents followed the basketball team everywhere they went.

My team was the first that had to be totally integrated. Before 1969–70, one could choose the school that they wish to attend. The

White schools could compete with the Black schools if they chose to do so. However, in 1969–70 school year, schools were totally integrated. However, as I stated before, we played in a time where there was an unwritten rule for basketball. My school was one that stated the coach could only have three Black players on the team floor at a time.

The best shooter on my senior year team was a junior. At the title playoff game to represent our district for the state championship, the principal thought that it was important to keep the schools scoring record in the hands of a White player that had graduated than to win the game to represent the district in the state championship tournament. The principal was sitting in the stands with who we found out later was the father of the White boy that was holding the school's scoring record of forty-two points.

The father and the other men of the White parents were all sitting together, watching the game together. Evidently, they were keeping the score of our individual scoring because as our leading scorer on the team had thirty-nine points. In the third quarter, the principal came out of the stands to talk to our head coach. I just so happened to be sitting beside the coach as I had just come out of the game for a few minutes rest and was told to sit by the coach as I was going back into the game very soon.

While sitting there, I guess to be able to hear what was said so that I could put the story in this book. I heard the principal telling the coach to take the leading scorer out of the game. The coach said, "What did you say?"

He said, "Take him out of the game, we don't want the scoring record to be broken."

The coach said, "But this is the game to go to College Park to play for state championship."

The principal said, "We don't care about that, take him out, he's a junior. We can try for the state championship next year."

The coach had to take the young man out or he would have been fired when we got back home. In those days, there was no three-point line. You could only get that many points by shooting two pointers and foul shots.

My team was a team! We didn't care who got the most points. We just wanted to win. I was the point guard, if someone was hot, we all would feed him the ball to win the game. The school record was forty-two points, and the young man had thirty-nine points in the third quarter. He could have gotten fifty points if he could have stayed in the game. He may have gotten fifty-plus points.

We still won the game but not because of the principal, we just played harder than the other team. One of the players on the other team went on to college and played on an all-Black team. His team won two or three division championships and he was on the team that played the NIT (National Invitation Tournament). He then went on to the NBA and played for the Seattle Supersonics.

Now, the change is on again. The White parents and coaches don't want the Black players on their teams as much. These people don't look at winning as they did before this era. They just want to see the White boys and girls on the field. They fill the stadium or field now just because their White children are being able to play. They now cheer as hard for their teams even when they are losing as they see the White children playing. When you hear them talking about the game now, you hear them say, "We played hard even though we lost. We will get them the next time."

In 2014, I took over a girl basketball team at a high school where the teams of all sports were losers. There was no school spirit. The fans laughed at the players for losing or making mistakes. I had a very young team. I had four seniors of which only I had ever played, two juniors that had very little on the court playing time, six freshmen that had never played before. As you might know, we lost most of our games, but I still encouraged the players and let them know that we would have our turn to beat teams. We lost one game 97–9. The principal came to me and said, "Good game, coach." I said, "What did she just say to me?" She was fine as she saw some White girls playing. This wasn't fine with me as I was a winner and came from winning programs.

The trend is now in the 2000s that the parents don't want Black athletes on their teams. As we look at our Little Leagues of football, soccer, baseball, the coaches are not putting the Black children on their teams.

They once went to playgrounds looking for Black children. Now, as you look, the teams are becoming all White. Win or lose, the parents don't care; therefore, the coaches are becoming of the same mind.

The Black children are still better at the sports, but the parents don't want them in their teams anymore. Why not? It was because they knew that the Black children were better, but if the Black children were in the team with their child, their child will not be able to play.

We as Black people need to pay attention to what is going on around us. I try to inform our young Black parents, but when they talk to the White parents, I am labeled as a troublemaker. I try to make the Black parents realize that their children are hanging on the street corners again. They are not doing anything constructive.

The White kids of their same ages are participating in some type of activity. A few years ago, in my area, there was an organization that had a Little League football program. For whatever reason, the program was losing kids. It was a White organization. Therefore, most of the kids that were playing were White.

First, the number of players on each team started to drop. Then the number of teams started to drop. The group started to look at the situation to find out what was the cause of the drop in participation. I did not know what they attributed the decline, but I do know what they did to change the direction that the program was going. As in everything in this country happens when there is a need to fix a situation, the group that is in trouble always come to the same conclusion. We will open the activity and offer it to the Black children. We will start to recruit the Black children.

They don't want us in the activity, but if they wanted to keep things going, we will have to include them. This has happened in this country on all levels; elementary, middle school, high school, college, and even it is moving to the professional level. Once the program is back in good standings, you will see less and less Black people participating.

I am sixty-five years of age and have been paying attention for a long time. I am a coach and have coached sports on all levels for over forty years. I still go to many sports events for the love of sports, but I am always watching for the changes in personnel on the playing field. I am old enough to have seen the world during segregation, when we as Blacks could not compete on the same field or arena with the White children. We only played together on sandlots. In my area growing up, when we played with the White boys, we always played Black vs. White. The Black boys won most of the games. We played together fine as long as the adults stayed out of our games.

As time changed, the White parents started to listen to their children, and then they started to ask the Black boys to play on or with their teams. As the teams competed against other teams and with teams from other neighborhoods, they were losing. The boys on the losing teams would tell their parents and coaches that if we had such-and-such on our team, we would win. This same thing happened in high school, colleges, and even the professionals.

Even more important to the White people was the money that they could make if they would put Black players in their team. They would see that by having the Black players, they would get the Black fans. Now that we have the Black players, we have the Black fans, we have more ticket sales. With the Black players, we are winning. Now that we are winning, more people are attending. We have pride in our team, and we are making more money.

In the Black community, there is less crime as now the young people have something constructive to do. The communities are safer, and everyone can relax. In all this, there came a problem. As coaches looked around at their teams more, they found that the more Black players I have, the more games I win. Everything about my team gets better.

As everything got better for the team, problems started to arise. The coaches a now recruiting more and more Black players, and this mean less and less White boys on the team. This trend became the norm for a few years. Everything was fine for years. Then the problem started to become stronger and stronger. The teams became all Black. The White boys started to complain to their parents more and more.

As the parents began to listen more and more to their children, they started to talk to other parents in their community more and more. The next thing that happened was the parents started to have meetings concerning this situation. As in everything else when it became a concern, the Black people in their clubs, the next step was to find out how to get rid of us. We were used to save the club when they were failing, but once they were back on their feet, they now don't want us around anymore.

In my hometown, when I was a boy, there was a public swimming pool in the marina. Once we found out about the pool, we started to use it as did the White people. Whether you knew it or not, the Black people in my area must had some type of contagious disease because if we got into the water with White people, they would get out. I guess they felt that they would get sick or something. As we used the pool, the White parents started to have meetings to keep us out of the public pool. The answer to the pool situation was to make a rule that the only way that one could use the pool was to have a boat docked in the marina. That solved the problem.

As I was talking about the football situation, let's look at what happened. I was one of the people involved with the young Black boys being added to the teams. At first, we thought that we could come into the league as a team to compete together, but they said no. They knew that if we were allowed to come in as a team, we would never lose. They said that we had to come in and be put into the draft.

It made all the teams to be even. The White players, coaches, and fans were happy with the addition of the Black players. The games became better and more exciting. The league started to boom. There were many more fans and even more teams. For this, you knew that the most important thing that happened was there was more money made.

The Black boys from my community developed more self-pride. The greatest thing for the Black boys was that before and after games, they were able to walk around our community with the whole uniforms on and show themselves to the people in the community what they were doing.

When the other young men of the community saw them, this made them want to play. The organization was very happy. Again, the success of the program once the Black players were there also caused problems. The teams were better, but as before, the players on the field were all Black.

This was true again, and there came meetings to stop the Black boys from playing. It got to the point that the White parents were trying to claim spots on the ground around the sidelines that were theirs, and no one else could sit there. I mean, everyone had to bring their own lawn chairs to sit in. Even if some Black parent or fan would get to the game before them and sit in a certain place around the field, the White fan would try to make the Black person move.

To move the Black boy off the teams, in the meeting, the White parents told the club that was sponsoring the league that they had to come up with a way to get the Black boys away. The solution to the problem was if you live over a certain amount of miles away from the playing field, you could not play. Well, that moved most of the Black boys as the club had moved the eligibility of the players to other areas far away from the playing field. They even were paying the buses to travel to the various communities to pick the Black players up.

Now that the parents had to provide transportation to and from practice as well as games, the boys had to leave the league. As I have stated earlier, the parents don't care about winning and losing as long as their children are on the field playing.

As I venture to the high school sports, I am finding less and less Black boys playing soccer, baseball, golf, and some other sports. There are less playing volleyball, lacrosse, and if they could, they would stop the Blacks from playing football. They are even finding ways to stop us from playing basketball.

The way that they are eliminating the Black players is the coaches are no longer putting Black children on their teams as children. You are finding more and more Little Leagues with all White teams. They don't go to the Black communities anymore to get the children to play on their teams.

Now when you go to high school soccer, baseball, volleyball, and lacrosse games, the teams are White. There may be one or two Blacks on some teams. You are now finding the Black kids hanging on the streets again. I always heard as I was growing up this saying,

"An idle mind is the devil's workshop." Here is when trouble starts in the communities. When children don't have anything constructive to do, the devil can put all types of bad behaviors in their minds.

If you pay attention, even professional sports are moving to foreign countries to put in Little League baseball and basketball. They are trying to develop the foreign children so that they can bring them to America to replace the Black children.

They are trying, but God has given Black people something that no one can take away. I see this country going to the place that it was in during the '60s. There were commercials that came on television where the Black people came on and said, "All we want is a chance."

The White man is doing all that he can to eliminate the Black people from everything. I hope that one day we as Black people will wake up and see how valuable we are to the world.

A few years ago, a situation came up where some White person said something about the Black athlete. I was trying to show the Black people how important they are. I tried to get the word out that if all Black athletes from every sport would go on strike or stop work for one day, the whole world would stop. We as Black people are in control of the whole United States of America if we would get on one accord and make our value known.

If we would say that no Black person will play their sport for one day, what would happen to the world? Some of you remember a few years ago when there was a Black man shot and killed in Baltimore City. The Orioles canceled their baseball games for two or three games. One could see what that did in Baltimore. Supposed every city would have done the same? Now that the professional team canceled their games, supposed high schools and colleges over the country forced their teams not to play to show solidarity for what had happened? The country would come to a standstill. Everything in the country would stop. The White man would try to continue on, but they could not without the Black players.

I was trying to make the professional Black athlete see that they didn't need the White owners to make them rich. There could be a Black league, and it would be just as strong without the White people. There were enough smart business people to run the league.

I didn't like the professional basketball player at first. However, I found out later that he is very smart. He had made Cleveland. Even when he was in high school, he was filling professional sports areas. The sports world try to make him look bad when he said that he was leaving Cleveland. Even I said, "Who does he think that he is?"

Well, my sons made me aware that when he left, he gave the Cleveland area two million dollars. When he said that he was going to have his own agent, I said, "Who does he think he is?" Then I found out that he paid the way for his friends to go to college to obtain the degrees needed to run his businesses.

The White man was mad as he was able to sit around and wait for a professional athlete to leave college and declare for the pros. When they could say that they will work to get them a lot of money to play pro sports, the professional basketball player said, "I am not going to make the White man rich, I am going to educate my Black friends to make them rich." I wish all the Black athlete would so the same!

Anything that the Black people used the White man for, we can obtain on our own. This may sound racist, but it is not. It is fact! The White man has always gotten rich from the sweat of the Black man!

At one time, a Black person was not allowed in White institutions. We had to go to the Black higher colleges for our learning. Once the White man found that by having the Black people in their colleges, they could make more money, that all changed. If the Black athletes, both male and female, would stop going to the big White schools and start going back to the historic Black colleges, those big schools would not be so big.

We hear the talk of the coaches at the big White schools as being geniuses. Well guess what? They are not. Who could not coach and win when you have all the best players? It was stated that Phil Jackson was an offensive genius in basketball. I say, was he a genius, or would you say having Michael Jordan on the team with the great roll players that were with him an easier job? Was John Wooden the great genius, or having Karem Abdua Jabbar and his people around him what made him such a success?

If these players were at a historic Black college with the Black coaches, they would have been doing the same thing. We were not smart enough to attend those big schools before. They didn't win all these games until they started to admit the Black players.

As I have gotten older, I have watched the teams go from "lily-white" to some Blacks, to more Blacks, to salt and pepper, to all Black. Now the trend is moving back. The big White schools, which are more diverse, are trying to become White again. The schools are able to do so by the Little Leagues not playing the Black children on their teams. Then the professional teams are moving their attention to trying to develop the foreign children more than developing the young Black children.

If the professional athletics don't start to pay attention and put the sports back into the Black communities, in the next ten years, Blacks will not be in professional sports. Blacks dominated most sports from the '60s to 2000s. Now as one looks, there are less and less. However, you always hear that the professional sports are putting their sport in foreign countries. You don't hear as much that they are putting their sports back into the inner cities where the Black children, both males and females, live.

You watch baseball now, and you see more White players than you have seen for years. There are a lot of foreign players also although they are not White. However, their color is of White. I don't know if people realize that any person that is foreign born is not White! They are people of color! Still, the man would rather have them than Black people.

I have watched colleges in my area go from predominantly Black to now much less Black and more White. I am watching as the White schools are keeping a lot of Blacks on their football teams in the skill positions. Then they are playing the Black players early in the game to gain the lead. Once they are leading by two or more touchdowns, they take the Black players out of the game. As long as they are in the lead, the Black players don't play anymore. If it should happen that the other team catches up, the coach will then put the Black players in the game as they know that the Black players can regain the lead.

The school also keeps their team in conferences that are mostly White. In this way, they don't have to compete with the schools that have mostly Black players. They go through their seasons winning most of their games again. Then they get into the playoffs and lose. The schools that are mostly Black still beat them as they have had to play tougher schedules.

When I go to watch the college teams that come to my area and play the team here that now is moving to the White boys again, there are enough Black players for them to compete as they only put the teams on their schedule that are predominantly White. The school in my area beat the body.

When the schools come in that have mostly Black players, this school is beaten hardly. The coach at this small division 3 school is Black. However, he let me know that the school has raised its GPA so high that the Black players cannot get in. Still, there are enough Black players there to allow them to beat most of the predominantly White schools that they play.

Another sad thing about the universities and colleges is that the schools are making money even on the players that are not superstars. What I mean is you can go into the school stores and find that they have the jerseys of players that don't play as much with the price tag on them almost as high as the player that is "superstar." The school is making money on every player, but the players can't get any pay for attending that particular school.

Again, the meetings that the officials have are mostly concerning the Black athletics. A player can go from Maryland to play on the other side of the country, make a lot of money for the school, but if a close family member dies back home, the school cannot give him or her money to get back home for the funeral.

The player may have eaten dinner at about 5:00 p.m. but get hungry late at night, the school can't give the player money to get something to eat. Still, that big school is making millions of dollars from what that player can do on the field or in that gym. Along with that, the school put the jersey in the window or on display and can make hundreds of dollars on that player's jersey.

When I was growing up, Black men could not be on the fire department crew. However, whenever there was a fire, the fireman would not move until they knew that this particular Black man was going to be where the fire was. There was one time that the house beside mine started to burn. There was an old lady that lived alone. When the fire trucks showed up, we the young people let the fireman know that the old lady was still inside the house. I know for sure the fireman did not attempt to go inside to get her out or not. Once the big Black man got to the fire, we told him that the lady was still in the house. We let him know that we had told the White fireman but they did nothing. The Black man ran to the door, kicked it open, and went inside to rescue the old lady.

In my area, sometimes our fire department would challenge fire departments from other places or towns in events. The one that I would like to talk about is the tug-of-war. As the fire department was all White, when they went to other places to compete with the other fire companies, they always came back as losers. Again, there were meetings to talk about the events for the next season.

As we stated, our fire company was always losers. At the meetings, they concluded that if they wanted to win, they would have to get bigger and stronger.

I heard the White cheerleaders talking on the bus when we went to away games. I would hear them saying such things as "I don't like a certain boy, but my mother told me to go with or date him anyway. His family got money. You go with him and even marry him, you may learn to love him. You just stay with him for that money."

They were not talking about the Black boys then. Still, they meant it for us also as we might go on after high school and become successful.

I have a nephew that attended a big White university back in the '90s. He was a track and football star. There were many White girls trying to be with him, but I want to talk about this one in particular. No matter where he would try to go after one game that we went to, she would turn up. She followed us all over the campus. Her father was upset, but her mother was right with her daughter to keep an inside place for him in case he went on to be a professional.

No, he didn't want her, but they didn't care, they were looking at the money!

All of you know what I am talking about. We used to say, those White girls would do anything that we ask them right in public just to be with us. All of you may want to get mad with me, but it is ok as you know that what I am saying is true. You know that you were called groupies.

Whenever you knew that the college or professional team was coming to your city, you would drop everything to go and be with them. You didn't care about how many other girls were with the same player. You just wanted to be with them also and would do whatever he asked. You would go to the places that you knew that they were going to spend the night and sleep on the street the day and night before just to be able to touch the players.

I coached at a division 1 university, but it was a lower level than the big schools. We didn't win many games, but I still learned what this word groupie meant. When we would get off the bus or plane in the area that we were going to play the next two days, these girls were there waiting for us.

Each player had three or four White girls with him, and they followed us around everywhere we went. I said to the head coach, "They are following us around and we are losing, what would it be like if we were winning?"

As I think back, this also happened on the high school level as I coached. I remember that I was teaching and coaching one high school team. I was the junior varsity head coach. My team won most of our games. We would always practice after the girls basketball team. As I would see my players walking around the school waiting to practice, they would be walking and would have four White girls walking with them. Some players had more, but most of the players had at least four.

Another way to prove this is by looking at America today. There are so many mixed children today. Let me tell you why there are so many mixed children today.

As I started to grow up, the schools were integrated. The White parents lied to their children and told them not to talk to or play with those Black children. They told them that we were bad and no good.

My father was a minister, counselor, and had attended college. He had a lot of wisdom. When we started to go to school with the

Whites, he said that there's going to be a lot of mixed children later. I asked him why he said that. He said that the lies that the White parents were telling their children were going to be proven wrong.

He said, "These children are going to be going to school from pre-kindergarten to 12th grade. The children are going to be interacting all day long every day. They are going to start to say, 'What my parents are telling me is not true.' The lies are going to cause the children to get together. I guess that the parents trying to keep their children away from the Black children is what caused them to be with the Black children more. They didn't realize that the more you tell someone not to do something, the more you are pushing them to do it."

As you go to stores, restaurants, and other shopping places, you see more and more of those "die-hard" White now grandparents with these mixed children.

Back to the sports, in my hometown, there were always public basketball courts once schools were integrated. Although I came from a small town, we always have very good basketball teams. The town kept us with basketball courts and kept them in good condition for the boys to play on. Now, as I ride through the town and look at the basketball court, I see that one rim and backboard is down, the ground has not been taken care of. When it rains, the ground has sunken so low that water stands on the court; when it dries, mud is all over the court and it cannot be used.

This is a plan as the town doesn't care about Black children. All other towns around kept the playgrounds and basketball courts in good condition. The plan is as before, if the Black children don't have anywhere to play, they will start to get into trouble again. Then, they can't play on the school teams and now the White children can play.

Still, the White parents don't care about winning. They just want their children to be able to play, win or lose. When I go to the games now, even if the children lose, the White people are okay. They say, "They played hard, and maybe we'll get them the next time!"

We don't have football at the school where I attended and still do not have football presently. When my boys came along in the '80s, they were both big kids. When my oldest son was in the 7th grade, he was over 200 lbs. My other son was in the 3rd grade, and he weighed over 100 lbs. I drove them to the next county so that they could play on the Salvation Army teams. There were three levels of teams there. My baby boy in the 3rd grade should have been on the peewee team. He was over the weight, so he had to play with the juniors league teams. He was in the 3rd grade playing with the sixth, seventh, and 8th graders. As it turned out, he was athletic and was a starter on the junior team. He played offensive and defensive tackle and also center. As he was a good player, the coach had the running back to go behind the block on my son, holes to gain yardage.

His team was undefeated that season. The team was 8–0 and won the league championship. From the league, there was an all-star team picked. The all-star team was going to Florida to play. My son made the all-star team as a 3rd grader on a team with 6th, 7th, and 8th graders. There were only so many players going per level.

If my son would go, this would knock this one boy that was in the 8th grade out. He was not as good as my son though he was in the 8th grade. Well, you know what happened? His mother started to fuss and complain for her son. She came to the meeting crying and everything as she wanted her son to go and play on the all-star team.

Everyone knew that her son was not as good as my 3rd grade son, but she wanted her son to play. She said, "My son had been play-ing all these years and have never made the all-star team. He is now having to move to the senior division and he is small and will never make the all-star team. I want you all to make my son an all-star. That Black boy is just in the 3rd grade, and he can make the all-star team many times."

Well, we were just a Black poor family and she was a White well-to-do family. Her husband was there, but he didn't say anything as he knew that this was wrong. Just as everything before, they had a meeting, and the White boy went and my son didn't.

You want to know what happened, well I can't tell you as I didn't have anything else to do with the league. I don't know how they did in Florida nor what happened the next year as I didn't let my sons play anymore. The league officials called me, but I didn't even talk to them. Again, they used my son to win the local championship, but then it was to move on, they left us out.

My oldest son was in the 7th grade and was a starter on the senior league team with players from 10th, 11th, and 12th graders. He played all line positions on both sides of the ball. I didn't allow him to play the next year either. Just know, when he was a senior, he had ten or twelve scholarship offers.

Later, I coached a high school team in the early nineties. We had a lot of success. We were in the playoffs several years. We won two state championships. That year, for some reason, the varsity team had a lot of White boys on the line on both sides of the ball. As there were meetings after every practice, we informed the varsity coach that this young man was real good. He told us that he was going to take him to the varsity team. I let him knew that he was not ready for that. He didn't care. He said that his boys on the varsity were not that good. The team the year before won the state championship and were mostly seniors. They graduated, and now he had a lot of White players that had sat on the bench.

He said that he was going to bring this boy up to put a fire on the now junior and senior White boys to make them work harder. He did, and you know what happened? The 9th grade Black boy moved up and was beating the older White boys in practice. While in practice, the White coaches were calling the older White boys all kinds of bad names as the young boy was beating them. There came another meeting after practice without me and the other Black coaches with the White boys and coaches. They made them feel so bad that in the next practice, they ganged the young Black boy on every play. They made it look legal so that we could not say anything.

When they started to beat the young boy, they started to call the Black boy names. The next day when we had practice, the Black boy did not come anymore. He quit the team. The coaches didn't care as he had made the White boys ashamed, and they started to play better.

The Black boy did not play anymore that year nor the next two years. He came back for his senior year as I talked to him every year to try to get him to play. I knew that they had stolen his joy and he was hurt. He came back his senior year and punished all the boys in the team. I don't know what happened to him as I left the school and went on to another state and became a vice principal.

I know that we are being used by the White world for our abilities, but the young Black parents and players can't see it. We as Black athletes can bring the world to a standstill, but we are caught up on what society is causing us to see. If we go to these big White schools, we can go to the pros for whatever sport. If we get one of these good agents, they will get me a lot of money from the pro teams.

The thing that these young players and parents don't understand is that wherever they go to school or who they get to be their agent, they are still going to be good. You, Black athletes, have the ability, and no one can take it from you.

The big White schools and agents started to track our young boys and girls in the 3rd grade. They sit around like vultures waiting for them to graduate so that they can make that easy money on our young children. You, young people, could go to the historically Black schools, with the Black coaches and be just as good or better than they are in the big White schools.

Let me tell you this, Black people, if the White people have their way, ten years from now, there won't be many Blacks in any professional sports. Let's look at baseball. The all-star game was on last night. There were a lot of nonwhites out there, but how many were African American? They were dark skin, but they were from other countries. The baseball world is sending money to foreign countries to develop the children there. How many teams are putting money in the Black communities to develop the young Black children?

Again as you ride over the inner cities, you are beginning to see the young Black children standing along the streets, but the White children are involved in constructive things.

You look at the softball, baseball, football teams on the Little League level, and the teams are becoming all White again. This is true in all sports. There are less and less American Blacks in baseball. As we knew, if the Black children are on the teams, we will dominate the sport. The White man is getting rid of us as Blacks in sports, and we are not paying attention to know it.

Writing this in a book won't help because as I was growing up, I heard it said if some information had to be put out and you didn't want the Black people to know, just put it in a book. They won't ever know because they don't read.

All that our young Black children want to do now is social media and video games. Once I get my book published, I am going to try to get this information out there through the social media. I need to sell some books first!

It was stated that in order to obtain this goal, we will need to put some Black men on our team. They never received the benefits that the firemen got of being firemen. Now, when the firemen would return home, they came back with first-place trophy from every event. If they could have done anything different, the Black men that were added to their roster would not have been there. They realized that years earlier, one of the Black men had been put in the ring to wrestle a baby gorilla. He lost, but it was said that the man was holding his own until the gorilla got tired of playing with him.

This talk of the strength of the Black man made the firemen decide to ask this man to be on their team for the next competitions that they would be in. Once the Black men were on the team, they won most of the events that they attended no matter where it was.

The same thing was true with the softball teams in my area. For the regular season, there were many softball teams. The teams would battle for the whole season. When it was playoff time, the Black team would usually win the championship. When the White team would go to other areas to play other teams, they would lose more than they would win. You already know, there would be another meeting. In that meeting, it was decided, "We have all these Black players in our hometown that beat us year after year. Why are we going to all the tournaments and coming home losers? We have some of the best softball players right here, and we come home losers. We know how to fix this problem, we will invite those Black players to be on our team when we go away to the tournaments."

Again, once the Black players were put in the team, they started to win championships. As with the fire department teams, the now softball teams were returning home with more softball trophies. I don't like having to say this, but it is true, White America doesn't like Black people. The real thing is they just tolerate us for whatever they can get from us.

This is true for my area to live, but if one looks deep inside, it is true over the country. You might say that there are many of us. Well, that is for the gain that they can get from being with a Black man or woman.

As I stated, I only attended high school with the Whites for my senior year. This became evident to me. As we the Black athletes of the school started to play our specific sport, the White girls started to stalk us. They would follow us around the school and would do anything that we wanted them to do for us. One or two of them even got pregnant by the Black boys. I had one to start to call me nights after school. She would not talk to me in school however. When we would play our basketball games, home or away, the whole school and community would be there.

It was said a few times, our town would be easy pickings for anyone that wanted to rob us as there was no one there if the basketball team was away.

The girl that would call me at night would be at the games also. If we won the game (we won most of them), she would make sure that she found me afterward when the crowd would run onto the court to congratulate us. When she got to me, she would grab me and kiss me.

Let me tell you a story. My baby brother had always been an athlete. Though he is nine years younger than I, when he was in the 7th grade, I always kept him with me. When I would go to play basketball with the men, I would take him with me. One day we were about to play, and only nine men had shown up. I put him on my team. He said, he couldn't play with us. I gave him a little pat on the butt and told him he will be fine.

From then on, he was able to play with the men even though he was significantly younger and not on our level completely. When he got in high school, he was the point guard on his JV team. In his freshman year, he led his team to a 19–1 record. The varsity coach moved him to the varsity team for his 10th grade year. He was now the starting 2 guard on the team. This team went 27–0. They won the state championship. The coach was also the physical education teacher for the school. He made my brother the gym assistant for the next three years.

The coach told my brother that all he had to do was come to the gym at the beginning of class to let him know that he was in school and then he could go wherever he wanted to go. This happened for all his years playing basketball. For the three years that my brother played for them, they only lost three games. After basketball season was over during his senior year, he was still supposed to be the gym aide. He went to class and did as he had done for the majority of his high school career.

Now that he could no longer play basketball and was basically no use to the coach anymore, this was an issue. He left class as always, and the coach called the office and told them that he was skipping class. My brother was called to the office and was given three days suspension. He was sent home and told not to come back. He told our mother when he got home. She reaffirmed that this was the same procedure he'd been following for three years now. She said that she would take care of it.

In the morning, she got my brother up, and told him to get dressed like every other morning. Once they were bathed, dressed, and had breakfast, they left to go to the school. They went to the school, and my mother asked to speak to the principal. When they got to talk to him, my mother told my principal that she needed the coach to be present as well. When the coach got there, she asked if my brother was the gym assistant. He told her yes. She then asked him if he had done anything different yesterday than he had for the past three years. He tried to say something different, but my mother was right to tell the truth about him.

She explained to the principal what happened and said that my brother was not going to be out of school for either day. She went on to mention that as long as he was playing basketball and the team was winning, everything was all right. Now that he was a senior and couldn't play anymore, the thing that he had been doing for years now had become wrong. She asked the principal if she was right, and he agreed with her. She then told my brother to go on to class and that would not be any more said about the matter.

Reader, I am again saying, do you love me, or are you just using me? You make your own judgment!

My Wilderness Experience

What does that statement mean? What exactly is a "wilderness experience"? When I first heard it, I didn't know what it meant. However, not only have I learned the meaning, but I've gained firsthand knowledge of what it is.

Looking back on probably the most known wilderness experience, I will draw my conclusions from the experience of Moses in the Bible. There was a job that God had intended for Moses to carry out. Most of the time, if God has a great experience in the works, there are great pain and obstacles that you must encounter and overcome first. This was the case with Moses.

The purpose for the great pain, shortcomings, and obstacles is to prepare us for whatever God has for us to do. How can anyone help others in their situation unless they have some life experience to draw on? How can you tell someone that God is a healer if you've never been sick? Or that he's a provider if you've never experienced need?

All of our experiences may not have been as hard or mind-blowing as that which Moses experienced in his life. He was put in a basket and floated along the Nile River alone. His sister followed along watching him in order to inform his mother what happened. If you know the story, he ended up in the home of Pharaoh. Pharaoh's daughter was placed in the right place at the right time for the journey to his predestined end to begin. She found him in the basket and took him home to rear as her own son. He was sent on the Nile as Pharaoh had commanded all the males of the Israelites to be killed as they feared that the Israelites would rise up against them and overtake them. They were in his words "more and mightier" than the Egyptians. Through the infinite wisdom of God, not only was he not killed, he also came up in the home of his enemy as the grandson of Pharaoh himself.

The beginning of his life showed that we can trust the wise ones who told us "The Lord works in mysterious ways," "What God has for you is for you," and "If God said it, that settles it!" No matter how long it might take, we can look back on his word and see that his words never return to him without fulfilling what they were set out to accomplish.

As Moses grew up in the palace, he received everything that the son of the king would possess. Through all this, he was even nursed by his mother. Since God had placed his sister in the position of servant to Pharaoh's daughter, when she was asked to retrieve a nurse, naturally she went to their mother. If there was something that God wants, nothing or no one can stop it. If God opens a door, no one can close it. And no one could close a door that he opens. The promise that God makes will come to pass no matter how long it takes. I may have to say this again and again in this book, as it is so true, God's will *will* be fulfilled!

When Moses grew up, he learned that he was not an Egyptian but was actually a Hebrew. When he found this out, he rejected all the good things that he had been receiving as the son of the Pharaoh. He went as far as killing a man for taking advantage of a fellow Hebrew. This started his official wilderness experience although the first part of his life could be considered a part of it as well. He was given a stick and sent out into the desert alone. Later, we will return for the rest of the story.

The story of my wilderness experience started on June 7, 1952. Just as Moses had a unique beginning to his story, so did I. When I was to be born, my aunt was the midwife and was present at most of the births in the Black community in my small hometown area. Women of color were not readily accepted into hospitals. They also could not afford the hospital bills even if they did accept them.

At the time, my mother went into labor with me, my aunt had been called to her bedside to do what she had done for so many mothers before mine. She was present and had examined my mother and determined that there was more time before she was to deliver. She told my mother that she was going to walk down the road and she would be back before it was time. To let it be known, she said that she was walking to her house a ways down the road, but she was really going to smoke a cigarette.

No sooner than she left the house, my mother told me that she yelled out for Miss Lily. As soon as she said that, I came out. This is reminiscent of the Israelite women during the time of Moses's birth. Pharaoh scolded the midwives because they were supposed to be killing the male children when they were born. "The midwives answered Pharaoh, because the Hebrew women are not as the Egyptian women; for they are lively, and are delivered ere the midwife come in unto them" (Ex. 1:9 KJV). When my aunt returned, I was lying on the bed. All she had to do was cut the cord. My mother always told me that my entrance made me special. I wouldn't find out until later that was the custom of my ancestors and that my birth was special really made it.

The earliest memory I have is when I was around five years old. One day, I was with my father and his brothers. For some reason, this day stands out in my memory more than others. It was winter, and there was a lot of snow on the ground. My uncles, my father, and I were being helped by some other gentlemen trying to free my uncle's car as it was stuck in the snow. They had tried several times to get the car out to no avail. I remembered saying to my dad, "Move over, Daddy! Let me help!" I put my hand on the car, and it was immediately freed. My dad said, "All that was needed to free the car was for you to touch it."

I decided in high school that I wanted to go to college to become a schoolteacher. I had watched two of my older sisters follow that path. They were elementary schoolteachers, and I wanted to carry on that legacy. I had also came into my athletic prowess during this time. I played sports in high school and was pretty good. In gym class and community sports, I was one of the better athletes in my area. Therefore, my mindset about going to college didn't change. My career plan did veer slightly. This sparked the passion to become a physical education teacher and a coach.

I graduated high school and went on to college as planned. I played sports in college but not for any of the school teams. They all wanted me to, but I moved away to college and had a girlfriend at home. I would go home to visit her almost every weekend as I had my own car. I did play various intramurals sports on campus. As I stated before, I was pretty good at sports, and we won several championships over the four years I played.

I started college in the fall of 1969, and in the fall of 1972, we had our first son. That basically ended me playing sports as now I had responsibilities to take care of. I found a job in college to make money for the care of my son. In 1974, my high school sweetheart and I got married! I went on to finish college with a major in physical education and minor in science.

I remembered going to the grocery store and seeing cans of seafood from my hometown. I saw that they were paying my mother and the other women in my community almost nothing, but the owners of the seafood houses were getting very wealthy off of their hard labor. Having the opportunity to get away from home allowed me to learn a lot about home that most people still there didn't know. God allowed me to get away and used something as simple as a trip to the grocery store to give me understanding of what was really going on so I could come back to tell the story.

I would go home on weekends and try to convince my mother and the other ladies who worked at the seafood house that they were being cheated. I told them that they should be making more money as the crab packers were getting rich off their backs. They were getting paid twenty cents for a can of crabmeat, and the packers were making between twelve dollars and fifteen dollars a can, depending on the type of meat. I told them that this was legal slavery that was being done to them.

I suggested that they go on strike and demand more money. I reminded them that other companies could find other people to fill in if their employees strike, but the seafood industry could not function without them. The packers would lose a whole lot of money because no one else could do the picking of crabs with the efficiency they did. The packers even had machines trying to replace the Black women, but they found the machines couldn't even keep up with them. They needed these women.

These women I was talking to had not been to other places outside our little community. They weren't able to see the prices that they were charging in other places for the product that only they could produce. When they would try to talk to other workers and the owners, they were told not to listen to me because I was a trouble-maker. The owners told the women that they could always come to them to borrow money during the winter when there were no crabs to pick. I tried to get them to understand that if the men paid them what they were worth during the summer, they wouldn't need to borrow money during the winter. That was money that would have to be paid back the next summer, keeping them in cycle of debt and dependence on the owners of the company.

I was privy to be in the company of some of the White packers to hear them say, "I make enough money from one day's work to pay my employees for the whole season!" Therefore, everything made from that day on was purely profit. When I relayed these things to the women, the lack of education and the lack of them seeing it for themselves would not allow them to grasp what was being done to them. All they could see was the winters were hard and their owners were good to them.

This is why slaves were killed for learning. They were hanged because the masters knew that if these slaves would become educated and start to think for themselves, they would realize one man as the overseer could not control the whole field of people working alone. This would lead to uprisings, and the slaves would be gone. As they would get free, they could tell the other slaves to do the same. They would help them, and they would go from plantation to plantation setting others free. There was a saying as I was growing up in the '50s and '60s, "If there was something that needs to get to the public but you didn't want the Blacks to know, put it in a book. They can't read, and the ones who can, won't!"

Once I graduated from college, I was able to get a job teaching in my hometown. I was still trying to make the women force the packers to pay them correctly. Soon after, I was let go from my job for no reason. The mayor of the town and the city council members for my hometown were the owners of the picking houses where the women worked. They knew that if the women listened to me, they would have to pay them whatever they asked for. That would have been fine, but they were so greedy, that was out of the question for them. To them, it was easier to get rid of me by forcing me to leave and get a job elsewhere than to pay the women.

As I look back now, this was the start of my wilderness experience. I realize this forty years later. I didn't know what it meant, but now I have come through it, and I have gained so much wisdom and knowledge. The greatest thing that I have learned is that though I was there, God was always with me. God has always stood by my side.

Now, let me take you on this journey that has been the last forty years of my life. This started in the year 1979, so it has been forty years exactly now. I was a schoolteacher in my county. Being as I had been labeled a "troublemaker," the officials of the town and the county commissioners decided to take my job. The city officials would not let any other seafood companies to come to the city as they said, "If other jobs come here, who will pick my crabs?" There were enough people in the city for two companies, but the greed was strong with them. They had the monopoly, and they were going to keep it that way. The county commissioners owned the farms, so they didn't want any other jobs. They wanted the Blacks to have no option but to pick crops for them. The Blacks were slave labor for the seafood companies and the farmers.

I had now been teaching for six years at this point. I have gained tenure and was certified for my position. There was a Black man on the Board of Education that was in charge of personnel. He was instructed to get rid of me though I had done nothing wrong. I soon became the project of this man. I was unaware that this was going on, so I was doing what I had been taught to do all my young life. I had graduated from high school, went on to college, started a career and a family. I did everything they told me was "the right thing" to do. Apparently, none of that mattered.

This assistant superintendent in charge of personnel was once the physical education teacher at the all-Black school in my hometown. He moved up to principal of that school before being promoted to the board. This same man was involved in several illicit affairs with female students as well as women on the Board of Ed. I knew this to be a fact as my sister was one of his victims when she was in high school. When she went on to college, he would leave our town to travel the two hours plus to go visit her at college. Oh, let me tell you! He was married! That didn't matter to him though. He loved my sister. He told my father if she would have him, he would leave his wife. It never happened, and my father told him that was not a good idea. My father was a minister, and he would never have gone along with something like that. My sister got married, and this relationship with this outside man made my sister's marriage unhappy. She finally stopped seeing this man. It was right at this time that he was to get rid of me as a teacher.

My wife and I were both working and bought a home. In our area, for Black people to get a home, car, or even a job, the Black people had to go to this man to cosign or as a reference. This was the time of integration struggles, and there had to be a Black person on every governmental board. Rather than the officials putting different Black people on each board, they put this same man on all the boards. That was their effort to integrate without dealing with "too many Blacks." What they didn't realize was that by using the same Black man on each board of the county, they gave him more power. Now, he could control everyone and could make the officials do what he wanted them to do.

I found out that he looked into my file as a teacher and found that I had done everything right in regard to my job. There was no ammunition that he could use to dismiss me. Instead of firing me, he found out that he could move me to another school. So my fifteen- to twenty-minute commute turned into over an hour each way. Now, my whole life and schedule had to be rearranged. I had to get up earlier and drive longer to get to work. This was all right with me as long as I still had a job.

During the summer, I worked as a teacher in the migrant program. This program was what it was called when the field workers came from Florida and Texas to pick the crops for the farmers in my area. The federal government gave the county money to teach the children of the migrant workers. Those children got more money than the families who lived in my county year round. The parents could send their children to school naked, but when they went home that evening, they were fully dressed and had extra clothes.

I worked at the migrant school as a teacher for several years. Every year in February, there was a convention. It was really a paid vacation for the teachers in the migrant program. One year, it was in Mississippi. My wife had left me prior to this trip. On the trip, I met a young lady from another part of the East Coast. We became friends and spent the week together. Once we returned to our homes, we talked on the phone, and she came to my city several times for the rest of the school year so we could spend time together. Overtime, we began a relationship.

The next year, the convention was in Philadelphia, Pennsylvania. We both attended the convention again, along with the Black man from my county. He had not attended the previous one in Mississippi. There were only three men in attendance for the whole convention. That was the man from my county board, another man from my county, and I. The three of us were sitting at a table together preparing to eat lunch. My significant other saw me and came over to my table to speak to me and let me know that she was there. I was happy to see her. I introduced her to the other men at the table. She gave me her room number. I told her that I would see her later, and we parted ways.

I explained to the men who she was, and we went on to eat lunch. Later that day, I went to her room. I knocked on the door, and she told me to come in. I went in and closed the door behind me. As I walked to her bed, I realized that she was crying. I asked her what was wrong.

She said, "I'm not a whore!"

I said, "I know that. Why would you say that?"

She informed me that my "boss" had been to her room and invited her to dinner. She asked him who he was. He said that he was my boss and that if she would go out with me, she should go out with him. She told him no again. He then told her that he hired me, and if she would not go out with him, he would fire me. She told him that he would just have to do that then as she wasn't interested in him. I told her that I was glad she did that. But guess what? He never said anything to me about it.

The next school year, however, I was moved to the school that was over an hour away, and I was fired from the migrant program. At the school that I was moved to, I was a long way from home. The school was from pre-k to 8th grade. I was the PE teacher and the science teacher as the PE teacher also taught science. The gym was also the cafeteria. The floor was a light brown or tan carpet. This man came to the school almost every day trying to get something on me to use against me to fire me. He went to the gym and saw stains on the carpet. He got the principal call the custodians to the office. He was trying to get them to say that the floor was caused by my neglect. They said that it wasn't my fault and that children spilled food and drinks on the floor. There were also after-hour events that could have contributed to it. They told him, "Mr. Ward doesn't even take his class out when it rains. That floor was like that before he came here this year."

There was nothing there that he could use against me on that trip. A few days later, he was back at my school again. I was called to the office, and the principal told me that a young lady said I looked at her funny when she came in the gym. I asked him what he meant. He couldn't say, but this was another way that the man was trying to get something to use against me that wouldn't work. The custodians told me what he had tried to do against me, and the young lady told me that he tried to make her say that I did something wrong. Neither of these things worked. I'm not through.

His next attempt was when he tried to use a White boy that had just moved to the school because he moved in with the family of a state police officer. He was a troubled child, and the officer was trying to help him. The man told the boy to bring a baseball to class. This was in 8th grade science class. As class was going on, the boy took the ball out and began to throw it against the wall over my head repeatedly. The other students in the class, which were mostly White with the exception of three Black students, asked him to stop so we could continue class.

He wouldn't stop, and finally I asked him to leave. I walked over to the door, about to call the office, and the boy got up and came over to me and proceeded to fall over the desk. He then jumped up off the floor and yelled out that I pushed him down. He then ran out and told the principal that I had pushed him down. The next day, the man was back. This time, he brought a county social worker with him. He was calling all the students in the class one by one to the conference room to ask them what happened. They all told them the same story I did as it was the truth. The students told me after the fact that he tried to get them to say that I did something wrong and became angry when no one would agree with him. Later, I was called down to the office and suspended for two days without pay. He made sure that went in my file, but I found out later it wasn't legal because I wasn't given a write up to sign. It did end up being removed from my file because it was false.

The final avenue he took was the last hired, first fired route. He told me that he was firing me as the county was putting all teachers in their own field of certification. Since I was the last PE teacher hired, I would have to go as there was no position for me in the county. Now, I told you that I was teaching PE and science, and there were other teacher teaching out of their field. But this only affected me. He moved another teacher from another school to my school to teach science. He took physical education out of the school and gave the classroom teachers an extra recess time and put that on the students' report card as physical education class. Yes, that was illegal, but no one said anything. Now, I didn't have a job as a teacher or anything else as the man had "blackballed" me from my job.

The superintendent called me at home one night and asked me to meet him at some place in town. He said that he wanted to talk to me. I went to meet him, and as we were talking, he started to cry. He said that there was no reason for me to not be working. There was nothing that I had done wrong to merit me losing my job. I said, "If that's the case, then why am I not working? You're the superintendent. You're over him. So, why don't you put me back to work?"

He told me that the man is Black and in a Black organization. "If I override him, he will sue me and say I'm not letting him do his job."

That was a poor excuse because if he had to go to court, the truth would come out that my job was taken under false pretenses. He said that he couldn't do anything because he had a family and could not risk losing everything.

Any place I tried to get a job after that was turned down because I had been blackballed. There was a supervisor position offered to me that I was well qualified for. I went through all the questions and passed all the tests needed to start the job. The company called for the top person in the company to come from another city to approve my hire. The plan was for the supervisor to come on Tuesday and for me to start work on Wednesday. The company called me on that Monday and told me that I couldn't be hired for the job because my ex-wife worked there. This didn't make sense to me as we were supposed to be on different shifts in different departments. I found out that when they called the board for a reference, they talked to the same personnel supervisor I had issues with. The very one who had blackballed me from the career path I'd spent my whole life trying to reach.

I tried to get unemployment to no avail. The same man told them that I quit my job. When you quit a job, you have to make over ten times what you made at the job before you can draw unemployment. This was a true catch-22. I tried to gain employment everywhere. I told companies that I would take a janitor job or anything they had available. I had a family to provide for. I was usually told that I was overqualified.

There was a new prison being built in my county. The prison board was looking for people to be teachers as they were going to educate the inmates. I applied and was readily accepted. I was a certified teacher. Not only could I teach the classrooms, I also had a degree in physical education, so I could run the gym and all recreation for the prisoners. My name was first on the list to be hired due to my qualifications.

As I told you earlier, this man was on every government board in the county. The prison board was also included in that. When they met and they were selecting teachers, of course, he was there as well. Once he saw my name, that was the end for me. At the same time I was also applying for the prerelease prison. My father told me that someone had blackballed me, so I should not tell anyone I applied for this other state job. We directed everyone to the prison in my county, and I ended up being hired at the prerelease prison.

When I started the job at the prison, I was informed the bane of my existence to this point had attempted to sabotage this job as well. The supervisor told me that he believed everybody deserved a second chance. I was a new hire, so it was initially a part-time job only. This wasn't enough to support a family, so I learned to shuck oysters. This was hard and dirty work, but it seemed to come naturally to me. Once I found my groove, I became one of the fastest shuckers in town. Though I was in the wilderness, things were going bad, but God was with me even when I couldn't see it.

Fast forward a little, an assistant basketball coach position opened up at the university in my county. This was a division 1 school. I played basketball against the new athletic director in high school. So when the job opened up, he called me and asked me if I wanted the job. I said yes, and I was hired. I was there for two seasons, and they were successful ones. We had the best two seasons that the school had in a long time. This was a part-time position. I worked there from October to March. I was paid a thousand dollars a month. I now had three jobs and still wasn't making what I was as a teacher.

At the beginning of what was to be my third season there, I went to the first day of practice, and everything was normal. The next day, the head coach came to me and informed me that the athletic director wanted to see me. When I got to his office, he told me that he didn't request to see me. I went back and relayed that to the coach. The next day, the same thing happened. I said to myself then that something strange was going on but continued on with practice. The next day, it's the same thing. Only this time, when I get to the AD's office, he told me that the president of the university wanted to see me. When I reached the president's office, I'm greeted with a handshake and a smile as if he didn't know why I'm there. He told me to come on into his office and have a seat. He started with small talk, but I got to the point and asked him why I'm there.

When I asked him why he wanted to see me, his facial expression changed. He looked as if he didn't realize it was me he was waiting to talk to. He and my father had been friends for a long time, and he was hurt and upset that he was about to deliver this news to me. He began to give me accolades on all the good things I've done over the past two seasons. He went on about how good I am with the team, students, and other staff members. Regardless of all that, his next words hit like a ton of bricks. He told me that I no longer had a position there as assistant coach. I asked him what I had done wrong, and he had no answer to give. I just didn't have a job anymore. I started to cry, but I didn't let him see and just walked out of his office.

I went back to the gym to talk to the AD. When I told him what happened, he seemed shocked. He then told me that he had a visit from a particular board member. Yes, him again! That the board member approached him if it was actually me that he had seen on the bench coaching at the end of the second season. He came to a game, saw me, and was told that I was doing a great job by a fan. The beginning of the season, he was at the AD's office after my job. The AD told him absolutely not. I was doing a great job and he had nothing to do with his personal issues with me. His next step was to go to the president. They ran in the same circles, and apparently his friendship with my father held no weight against this board member.

Let me tell you...this man has some serious issues with me. After my sister stopped dating him and he was turned down by my girlfriend, I became his archenemy, and it was like his life mission was to make me miserable. Being rejected by my girlfriend, a mere teacher, was too much for this man's huge ego to take. And that she would not only reject him, but in favor of me was adding insult to injury.

Now, I'm out of one of the three jobs that I was working. As if it wasn't hard enough trying to support my family with all three of them. Soon, oyster season will be over, and all I will have was the part-time job at the prison. I'm working only part time with a wife and two children to support. It didn't take long before my wife decided to leave me. She left while I was at work and took everything. And I mean everything! She even took the curtains from the windows. The only thing she didn't take was my children. They came home from school just as shocked as I was.

Okay, so she and her paycheck were gone, and I still have myself and my two boys to provide for. I was able to get a job for the summer working seasonal work in seafood at the same place where I shucked oysters. We were able to get by with the help of God and my parents. "Surely the Lord will provide!" I was able to work all summer at the job in soft crabs and the other seafood. I was even able to get my boys a job working with me at the same company. I was still teaching them about life as they also had chores to do at home. They had to keep their rooms clean and help keep the house clean. They also had to cut the grass.

My boys didn't like to cut grass, so I told them that if they didn't want to cut it, they could pay me twenty dollars a week and I would cut it. I actually loved to cut my grass and wanted it done the way I wanted it cut anyway. I wanted to teach them responsibility with their money. We worked all summer, and they saved money for their own school clothes. I also kept the money that the paid me for cutting the grass to add to their school clothes fund.

It's now time for them to go back to school, and the job also ended for me. I still had to provide for them. So, I went to the fields to pick crops. I found myself in the cucumber field and then beans. As a boy growing up, I would pick tomatoes, strawberries, and beans. I was good working the fields. I could pick one hundred quarts of strawberries per day, but that only pays ten cents per quart. I could pick seventy-five to eighty baskets of tomatoes per day consistently. Some days I could pick up to one hundred. That paid twenty-five cents a basket. I was never good at picking beans, so I rarely went to the bean field.

Still, I found myself as a man in the fields picking crops with a college degree. I tried to get a job with the police department in my hometown. That was a no go. I was always told that I couldn't pass the lie detector test. They told me that I was lying about using drugs. I'm quite sure I knew better than anyone whether I used drugs or not. I found out later that they were in on me being labeled a troublemaker.

Things had come to such a bad point I found myself walking my dog around picking up soda bottles to turn in at the store for food to feed my children. The store owner would pay you at that time a nickel for each bottle. I could usually gather enough to get at least bread and bologna. I would have potatoes but no green vegetables. I remembered going into the fields at night trying to pick greens for us to eat. The only problem was that I didn't know the difference between greens and weeds. At times, I had taken grass or weeds home to cook for my family.

At this time, my oldest son was in the 4th grade. Wouldn't you know that this board member showed up at his school? My son came home one day and told me that a board member called him out to talk to one day. He went on to tell me that the strange man put his hand on his head in front of the classroom full of students and asked him if I was his father. When my son told him yes, he said, "I sure took care of your daddy, didn't I?" Of course, my son had no idea what that meant, but I certainly did! I went to his office to confront him and tell him not to bother my child ever again. That was the end of that.

School has started, and I'm in the field picking beans. The pay for beans has drastically increased since I was a boy. They paid fifty cents a hamper when I was little. Now, it was ten dollars a hamper. To fill a hamper with beans was no easy feat though, so it may have been worth it. The hampers were twice the size of the baskets we used for tomatoes, and the beans were so small you have to pick many, many more beans than tomatoes to fill the hampers.

I was so embarrassed to be picking beans that because I knew the school bus would come past the bean field, I would park my car way down the fields so that the children wouldn't be able to see my car. When the bus would come past me, I would lay down in the field with the wet vines and the ground muddy from the dew. It would take almost all day to get dry.

One time, after being in the field almost all day, I stopped and looked around. I looked at all the people in the fields working along with me. There were migrant crews in the field with me. They came mostly from Florida and Texas every year to work these fields. Most of these people move from place to place with a crew leader. This was the boss who contracts with the farmer to pick the crops for the season. He then instructed and supervised his crew for the duration of the season until it's time to move to the next location. Because he was responsible for making the contract, when the farmer told him he paid ten dollars a hamper, he took five off every basket, and that's how he made his money.

Since I'm working on my own, I will receive the ten dollar per bushel rate. I looked at the same hamper I started the day with, and it was not even close to full. I started to look around to see how the others were coming along. I looked around, and other people had full baskets behind them. When I looked behind me on my row, I saw multiple full baskets. I asked the owner of the field if my row was the turn row (the row where the hampers were placed to await pickup), and he told me no. I'm stunned because I knew that I've been working on this same hamper all day, and I had no idea where those other baskets came from. I walked back and counted twelve baskets full of beans. I was puzzled to see this. Then I said to myself, "The Lord put these here!" I had seen a miracle before my eyes! I told the Lord thanks as I went to collect my $120.

You knew in the book of Job, Satan presented himself before the Lord, and God asked where he'd come from. He responded, "Walking to-and-fro on the earth, seeking whom I may devour."

To which the Most High replied, "Have you considered my servant Job?"

The adversary told him that there was no need to test Job because he already knew he was protected by God. God told him that he could take everything he had, only not to touch his body. Job withstood the test and continued to praise and trust in God in the process. I have been told by many people in my church that I am like the servant Job. God allowed him to take everything away from me except my children and my health.

Before I could make it back to my seasonal job at the oyster house, I lost my love. My beautiful, mint green 1977 Chevrolet Monte Carlo. I was able to go to a man who sold cars for weekly payments. My payment was twenty-five dollars a week. They were payments I could afford to make sure that my children and I had transportation. However, one day after work at the oyster house, I cleaned up my area and was leaving to go home. I went outside to my car, but it wasn't in the parking lot where I left it.

Naturally, I was beginning to get upset as I didn't know where my car was or what was going on. One of the men in another department told me that some man in a truck came and took my car. I was hurt again. If all those men saw someone come and take my car, why wouldn't they tell me? Instead they waited around for me to come out so they could laugh at me. I had just gone through this with losing my beloved Monte Carlo. The process was the repo letter went to the sheriffs departments pick it up. They had a notice to pick up my Monte Carlo but never came to get it. The only one who would come to my house to get my car was my cousin who worked for the sheriffs. He thought that it was funny to take it, but I could do nothing about it. Family usually are the worst ones.

Through all these things, God was still with me. I got a notice one time that I was about to lose my house. I got down on my knees and cried out to the Lord while my boys were in school. I told God that I needed his help because I didn't have money, but I needed a place for my boys. When I spoke to the landlord to try to explain, they said I was all caught up! I didn't know how this was possible because I had missed at least three payments. Even in the wilderness, God was with me. This happened with the electric bill as well. Once again, I called to make a payment arrangement, or ask for more time, only to be informed that my payment was current. I was seeing the supernatural provision of God in action.

After I lost the second car, I came into contact with an older couple. This couple had a car but had been restricted from driving because of automobile accidents. They put the car up for sale for $300. My father bought it for me. This way I would have reliable transportation for my family that no one could ever come and take away.

A few years before this, I had started having strange experiences. I had a dream one night, or maybe it was an out of body experience. What I knew was I was asleep and then suddenly there were six white doves that came to me. They picked me up and carried me to some place where there were chandeliers hanging down. I didn't know where I was, but they flew me around in the place among the chandeliers. I was flying very fast through them, but I never hit either of them. After they flew me around for a while, they took me out of the area and allowed me to see where I had been. Then a voice said, "I am carrying you!" The birds carried me back to my bed, and I saw myself lying there before they placed me back in my body. When I woke up the next morning, I remembered what happened, but I didn't understand what it meant.

From the time that my wilderness experience began to the end, my ex-wife left me a total of three times. When she had been gone for eleven months, and I thought I was done crying and over with the situation, I got a new girlfriend. My life seemed to be going pretty well considering I wasn't a teacher anymore. I had begun to consider myself an alcoholic. I was never a big fan of liquor, but I loved beer. If I had one, I had to have at least six. I could ride around with a cooler full of beer and drink every one of them by myself. I didn't need any company to drink my beer. I had fun all by myself!

To my astonishment, my ex-wife just decided one day that she wanted to come back. I told my parents that she was saying that the boys missed me and needed their father. I knew that I told you that she left them with me. About six months later, I was working three jobs and getting home around one in the morning. I would leave them with my parents while I was working, but that meant that I had to wake them up in the middle of the night and turn around again and get them up again in order to make it to my morning job. I eventually talked to their mother and informed her that I didn't think the boys were getting the rest they needed and that it would be in their best interest to be with her. They didn't want to go, but they did go to stay with her. I still took care of them. I made time to visit and talk to them almost everyday. She didn't have to spend any of her money on the kids. I gave them money so that they didn't have to ask her or anyone else for anything. I was far from a deadbeat dad even though we didn't live in the same household.

But now she wanted to come back and try to be a family again. I took her back, and a few years later, she left again. She would have extramarital relationships and had no respect for our marriage or me. Her boyfriends would have the audacity to call our home phone and ask me to speak to her. As if I was her butler or answering service! She went out on the weekends and told me she was "going out with the girls." I had a fellow teacher who moonlighted at a local hotel. She came to me one Monday morning detailing how she had seen my wife with some man (who clearly wasn't me) all weekend at the hotel where she worked. The last time she left, I said I wasn't going to allow myself to be hurt by her again. As soon as I would begin to heal and start a new life, she would hear how happy I was and inevitably she would be back at my door.

Now, it's about seven years after I lost my teaching job. There was a Black man accused of killing a White girl in my community. The police had no proof or anything to go on to accuse this man of the murder except he was in a relationship with the girl at the time of her death. They arrested him and beat him until he gave them a false confession about the murder. The mother of this same man went to Baltimore to obtain a Black lawyer for him. When he looked at the case (including pictures of her son after the beating), he agreed to take the case. He walked into the courtroom and demanded that the judge dismiss the case for lack of evidence and a coerced confession. Once the judge looked at the pictures and heard the lawyer's argument, he immediately dismissed the case.

When I heard what the lawyer did for that young man, I reached out to the newly vindicated man's mother and got the lawyer's information. I contacted the lawyer and explained the situation with me and being wrongfully terminated and blackballed from the education world. He asked me to come to his office in Baltimore so we could talk in person. My brother took me to meet with him. After going over the details of me losing my job, he told me he was confident that he could help me. All he asked for was $1,000 retainer. The rest of his fee was to come out of the settlement. He came and investigated in my hometown and surrounding areas and told me that he was going back to his office to write up and file papers for a thirty-five-million dollar lawsuit against Somerset County. He didn't get into any details of what he had uncovered, but he went back to Baltimore and got right to work. He was sending out subpoenas and taking depositions. He would call and give me updates, and when I would call him, everything was fine. I was excited! Was this the moment I had been waiting for?

Then everything changed. Big shock, right? Now when I called, I could not get him on the phone unless it was to ask for more money. The first time it was $1,600. My wife and I borrowed the money, and I took it to him. Maybe six months later, it was $1,800. My whole family came together to get that money together. With all the assurances I was given and the way we had seen him work on that young brother's behalf, we had the utmost confidence that this money was an investment. In spite of the fact that initially we were told that the retainer was all he needed.

When I didn't hear from him after taking him the second retainer, I went to his office in Baltimore unannounced to see him. He had the audacity to ask me for another $1,800! I told him that I couldn't come up with anymore money and that we had an agreement that didn't involve any more money until there was a settlement. He said that he couldn't represent me anymore without any more money, but if I could come up with it, he was ready to go to trial. He told me that some lawyers from Somerset County would be calling me for a deposition. If I didn't come up with the money, he would not be able to accompany me, but for me to not say too much, when I went. What was too much? I wanted to tell them the truth! I pleaded my case in the deposition so they knew everything that I was going to say. I never heard from the lawyer again.

The next call I got was from an overly friendly Somerset County judge. He informed me that he was presiding over my upcoming case. He said that there were two ways my case could be carried out as the date was fast approaching. I could have a jury trial a month from then, or I could go in front of him alone in a week. It was my choice. I asked him to explain the difference. He said that I could come and present my case to him and let him make the ruling, or I could go in front of a jury. That would take much longer, and I would have to go through jury selection. Now, I had no lawyer and no money to get another as I'd given my lawyer a total of $3,400, and he abandoned me. The judge and lawyers knew that I was desperate, so they made me feel like this was the way for me to go.

I didn't know anything about the law or courts, and at this point, I had no one to advise me. If the judge was really seeking justice, he wouldn't have pressured me. However, he was in league with the Board of Education and the "good old boy's club." He knew my financial state from the deposition and used it to persuade me that a bench trial was the best thing to do. I called my lawyer to let him know that we had a court date for the next week. No response. So I'm headed to the district court in Baltimore without a lawyer.

The right thing for the judge to do would be to advise me against proceeding without council. The trial went on as scheduled. I'm standing there with no real knowledge of what my lawyer found that he thought made this case such a sure thing for him. All I had was the list of subpoenas from my lawyer and my inside information of the case to go on. When I begin to question the board members, it quickly became obvious how this was going to go. Every question I asked was answered with no variation I don't remember or it was too long ago. It became apparent that the judge and lawyers had already gotten together and discussed my case. There were ten men that I had to question in total, and every one went the same way. That was the entirety of my case. The defense offered no argument as there was none needed. My own witnesses had destroyed my case.

The courtroom was empty, with the exception of the people for my case. The judge said that he would go on to make his ruling. It didn't take him long at all to say that there was no evidence to prove my case, so it would be dismissed. I heard my father's voice from behind me saying, "Come on, Bern. You see what they did!" As we were leaving, the lawyers and the members of the board were shaking hands and celebrating their victory. We left the courtroom to start the long journey home, feeling defeated.

A few days later, I sat down and wrote a twelve-page letter to the lawyer's grievance board for Maryland, detailing the actions of my former lawyer. An investigation was opened into the lawyer's actions. He was eventually disbarred from practicing law in the state of Maryland. Yes, he was disbarred, but what good did that really do me? My case was over already. The crazy thing about the whole story was that he was found dead not even a year after this whole case fiasco was over, and it was all kept hush-hush. I had a cousin who lived in Baltimore and knew the family of the lawyer personally. They said that the family never talked about his death.

A few years later, I found out what the big secret was that made my case such a sure thing for that now deceased lawyer. At the time I was being persecuted and ostracized, there were a bunch of White teachers in Somerset County who were teaching without degrees. The Black teachers during that time had to pass the NTE, or we couldn't graduate until we did. The county had a "good ol' boys" system, so degrees were not necessary for some. What they could do before integration in 1969–70 school year was go to college, usually Salisbury State for one or two years until a position opened up. Then they would leave with whatever credits they had attained and started teaching.

This was allowed before integration as the superintendent of schools was one of them. The thing that they were doing was the teachers would teach until they were ready to retire. When they were ready to retire, they would have one of their children or relatives take a few courses, and they would place them as their replacement when they retired. This whole system began to deteriorate when total integration came to our county. The Black teachers who were coming into the school system now were certified, opposed to the White ones who were grandfathered in. We could bump the White teachers out of their positions as they made sure that we all had been certified before we were allowed to teach.

The crux to my case was the fact that I was a certified physical education teacher with tenure. I had been told that the county was letting all teachers go that were not certified, and certified teachers were being given positions. I was told that I was the last phys ed teacher to be hired, so I was being let go because all the other teachers had certifications and had been teaching longer than I. The fact of the matter was that the boy's PE teacher at Crisfield High School was not certified, he didn't even have a degree! He had only been to college for two years, but he was a friend of another teacher in the county. He had been brought there all the way from West Virginia because the county didn't want to hire the Black PE teacher from the Black school to teach at their newly integrated, formally all-White high school.

The phys ed teacher at the White high school was moving from the PE teacher to become the principal at the now integrated high school. I'm just realizing thirty years later, at the time of this writing, that the man that was made the principal may not have even had his degree. The principal of the Black high school had to have his degree, or he would not have been allowed to teach or be the principal before integration. When the schools came together, the Black principal was moved to the Board of Ed. as assistant superintendent in charge of personnel. (Yes, him!) He was given this position so that he would not want the position of principal at the White school, and they could put their man in there.

Now let me tell you what happened. I was fired, no matter what they called it. I was fired. The grounds for letting me go were fraudulent, and my lawyer had uncovered that. There was at least one PE teacher that was not certified and didn't have a degree, but they kept their job while I was let go. Later, I found out that when the board member (that one) learned that I was going to sue the county, he got involved because he knew that I would have won my case, and we would have been the one to take the fall, being he was the only Black person involved and he was the one who actually fired me.

It's been alleged to me that this man was friends with the president of the NAACP for the state of Maryland, and he spent a lot of time in Baltimore. He allegedly went to this friend of his for help in finding a way to stop me. Totally disregarding the fact that his mission was supposed to be the uplifting of his fellow Black people, he was not against conspired with one man of color to destroy another brother. They conspired together with my former lawyer to milk me out of my money so I wouldn't be able to afford him when the time came for the trial. I believed that once my letter got the lawyer disbarred, they feared that the lawyer would expose them, and that's why he ended up dead months later. This man from the NAACP is now the pastor of a large church in Baltimore and a government official. My life is still in the wilderness. Life has gotten a little better, but I have been suffering with undiagnosed depression since 1980 when I lost my job, and there was no justice from it.

Fast forward to approximately 2003, I was singing at a funeral, and a man I'd never met before came up to me and said, "God wants to bless you." I didn't pay him any attention really. He said it again. His wife was with him, and I recognized her. She introduced me to him and informed me that he was the principal at a large school and that he wanted me to come to his high school to be one of his assistant principals. I resigned from the teaching job that I had and took the job, which was in Chester, Pennsylvania.

By this time, I had reconnected with and was remarried to the love of my life. My wife worked at the airport, and that meant I could fly for free. So being that I lived almost three hours away from my new job, I took advantage of that perk. I would fly to Philadelphia, and there was a bus that I could catch to get to Chester. This was another way I could see the hand of God in my wilderness experience. Even if you aren't going through negative things in our lives at the time, we have to learn to trust God. The Bible said, "God will never leave you nor forsake you." No matter how hard my life got, I knew that God was right there with me, and that was how I made it through my wilderness.

I worked at that school for the remainder of that school year. This school was in a very bad condition when I got there. It was the only public high school in the whole city. There were many gangs in the school who were always at odds and causing problems. Whatever went on in the community always got brought into the school. We had armed security officers in the school and metal detectors at the doors. There were still times when they would get guns in the school. Students would sometimes put guns outside of the rear doors without detectors. Once they would get into the school, they would go to the door and open it as far as they could and bring the gun into the school. There was some type of weapon found in the school almost every day. The school was not allowed to have fire drills because inevitably, there would be a fight between the gangs.

I entered into this new job totally unaware that because if all the issues going on, the state was about to take over the school. I had received tenure at the school I was teaching at, but I had only been at this school for a year. I was the last teacher hired at this school, so when the state took over, I was let go. This was really frustrating to me as I had finally got a good job teaching, and I let that go to work for this man. It was almost time for the next school year, and I had not heard anything about a new job.

I contacted the superintendent from the school in Chester and let him know that I left my good job to help the principal in his school, and now I'm left without a job. He agreed with me that the situation was unfair and told me to expect a call in the next few minutes after we hung up. Sure enough, not five minutes later, my phone rang. The lady on the other end asked me if I would be able to come to Prince George's County in two days to meet with her. She gave me the specifics of where I needed to meet her, but that was all the information I had. I arrived two hours early as I had given myself extra time in case I got lost. Résumé in hand, suit and tie on ready for an interview, I made my way to the front office. The receptionist directed me to her. When I approached her, she greeted me with, "I told you to be here at four. I have a school to run."

While we were talking, two boys came into the office as they had just been in a fight. I didn't know anything about them or the school policies. That didn't matter to her; she told the boys to go with me and told me to handle the situation. I was shocked, but I went along with it. I took the boys to the cafeteria and handled the situation. By the time the principal came back, the issue was resolved, and the boys were friends again.

When 4:00 p.m. hit, she then called me to the office along with one of the vice principals. She asked me to have a seat. I pulled out my résumé, preparing to go through an interview. We talked for a few minutes, but there were no "interview" questions asked. She asked me if I knew where the board office was. She gave me directions as I was unfamiliar with the area and told me to report there in the morning. This was on a Wednesday afternoon. Initially, she said that she wanted me to come in on Friday, but she told me before I left to show up for work on Monday morning. I left her office puzzled and wondering what had just happened. I knew this had to be an act of God because not only was I not interviewed for the job, I hadn't even applied for it! All I could say was, "Thank you, Lord!"

I taught in that school for twelve years. I enjoyed being there. It was actually a great school. It was nothing like I had expected. The students and staff were great! I lived two and a half hours away from this job. I didn't want to move my wife to that county as it was too fast, and it wasn't a good area. Where we lived, we could go out and leave our doors unlocked and not worry about anybody taking anything. Even though I was making more than most principals made in my area to teach phys ed here, the cost of living was extremely high there. It made more since to be financially to make the good money up there and bring it back home where it was worth much more.

I told you that I didn't even apply for that job and that I knew it was God who gave it to me. It started to become a blessing and a curse. I had thirteen car accidents over the years that I worked there. A total lost of five cars in those accidents, but I walked away from every one unhurt. At each accident scene when the cars were totaled, the police always asked if I wanted to go to the hospital. There was never any need, but there was no way I could drive either of the cars away from the scene.

One of the accidents I got into, I wrapped my car around a pole. I was in a couple's yard. They came out to find out what the noise was and found me still in my car unharmed, and my car literally wrapped around the pole. The lady ran to me and told me to get out of the car in a hurry because the gas tank was leaking. She said that my car may blow up. The car didn't blow up, but the traffic on my side of the highway was backed up for six hours.

Another one of the accidents I had, I ran a red light and hit a van. My car spun down the highway and came to a stop on the median. This was at night, so I couldn't see the damage done to the car. The tow truck came and pulled my car off the scene. When I got to see my car when I went to get the stuff out, I almost passed out. Hitting the van caused my motor to twist so that the motor was sitting beside me in the car. My lunch box was smashed to the seat, and

I couldn't get it out. It was trapped by the motor. If there had been a passenger in the car, they would have been smashed to death. The car looked really bad, but to look at the car on the driver's side, you wouldn't even be able to tell I had been in an accident.

The final accident I had related to this job, I wasn't even driving a car. I was working bus duty, and the bus had stopped to let the children get off and go inside the school. The flashers were on, and I was standing with my hand up asking the drivers to stop as the children were getting off. There were two lanes for the children to get into the school. There was a lane for the parents to let their children out and then the bus lane. No parents were to be in the bus lane. One of the parents ran right into me. The teachers asked the lady if she knew she had run into me. She responded with, "I know. He was in my way and I don't have time to wait!"

The principal sent me home and told me to go to the hospital to make sure I was okay. From there, I was sent to see a psychiatrist. The accident had caused me to develop PTSD. My mind was on overalert. I could not go back to school until I was cleared by the doctor. They were afraid that I would see a fight and overreact and possibly hurt one of the students.

During this time, my wife and I had a meeting with a man who was trying to sell us something. We told him that we were not interested. He continued to press us as that whatever he sold, he would get a commission. I had told my wife prior to this that I needed her to keep an eye on me. If I began to act strange, I asked her to check me and get me away from the situation. As we were talking to the man, I said that I was done. She said okay and continued on with the conversation. The man took it too far and had the audacity to raise his voice on my wife. Before I realized it, I was going across the desk to hit him. My wife told me to stop and leave the room. Nothing was worth all that.

I have stated before that I have three sons. The two that I raised will be who I'm talking about. In the year 2005, my middle son was thirty years old. He had spent eighteen months of his life in the penal system earlier in his life. He had been out for several years at this point. He had a girlfriend or two and was doing all right with his life.

One day we were standing outside talking to his mother. We were both remarried at this time. Even though the children were grown, we still remained cordial for them. She asked him what was wrong with his leg because she had noticed that he was limping. He told her that there was nothing wrong, he was just trying to keep his pants up because he didn't have a belt on. This whole sagging craze was one I'll never understand.

Later that night, we heard that he had an accident. He was on the highway and the police told me that they were trying to stop him for speeding. Though he was trying to stop him, he continued to go faster. He was going so fast he couldn't make the turn in the road and ran off the road across a ditch and hit a tree.

When he was in high school, he played football and lifted a lot of weights. He should have played on an offensive or defensive line, but his coach made him a middle linebacker because he was so athletic. He had continued to lift weights and play football and received scholarship offers to play football in college. He didn't take any of the scholarships and even quit high school. He got a girl pregnant while he was in high school, and they had a little girl. Once he went to prison, he continued lifting weights, so he stayed big and strong. He was about 290 lbs.

Going to see him in the hospital, he didn't look as badly hurt as I expected when I heard about the accident. The doctors told us that he would be starting rehab very soon. He had now been in the hospital for about a week now, and we thought he was getting better. When anyone visited him in the hospital, he made sure he apologized to them. He was asking for forgiveness for anything he may have done to anyone. Whether he knew he was about to leave this earth or not, no one knew. It sure seemed that way in hindsight.

We found out that the limp that fateful day was the beginning of some type of ministroke he had. His left leg from the knee down was paralyzed. This was why when the police were chasing him, he kept accelerating. He said that he thought he had taken his foot off the gas, but he didn't. I asked him one day if he could move his legs. He lifted his left leg in the air then went on to say, "Look, I can move both my legs. I'll be out of here soon starting my rehab!" His right leg never moved. I was scratching his leg and even pinched it really hard, but he never felt any of it. I didn't tell him, but now I knew what the police said was true.

On Thursday morning, my older brother called me from his home in New Jersey to check on my son. I told him that he was improving as of the night before. He said that he was on his way to see him. I told him that I would meet him there. I was about to leave to go to the hospital when the phone rang. It was one of the nurses. She asked me what I was doing and said she called to inform me that my son had a seizure. I told her I was on the way. When I got to the hospital, his mother was laying over his face. I heard one of the people in the room say "Here's Bernard." She rose up and turned to look at me and said, "Our son's gone" I fell right in the floor. The next thing I knew, people were helping me up off the floor. I was so confused. The nurse just said he had a seizure. I realized that she didn't want to tell me all that over the phone.

I was now learning that when he was in the hospital after the accident, the doctors checked him for internal injuries. What they didn't tell us was that he had been completely eaten up on the inside with cancer. Evidently, he had cancer, and it was dormant. The impact from the accident caused it to mestastasize throughout his whole body. We didn't even know that he had cancer. I found out that he had been smoking since he was twelve. If he knew that he had cancer or not, we didn't know. With a lot of people, they didn't tell their family that they are sick until it gets so bad that they have to tell them. Evidently, it never got that bad for him.

We found out later that he had gone to his girlfriend's house and told her and his daughter that he was sick. The blessing in this, if there is one, is that in prison, he gave his life to Christ. Whether in jail, or in a church, it's just as meaningful. You are his regardless. With the way he was making amends, it led me to believe later that he did know he was sick. I spoke and sang at his funeral. I told his friends that even though they may not understand, Kenny was all right. "You must do the same one day. Don't think this is too early to die. Anyone can go at any time, and if you want to see Kenny again, you must find peace with the Father through his Son."

I had some people ask me after how I could find the strength to talk and even sing at my son's funeral. I told them that I'm saved also, and I knew that I will see my son again.

Life has gone on, and I have been a very lonesome man. Not only from losing my son, but the combination of all the things that had transpired over this whole wilderness journey. Remember I told you I was out on medical leave for my mental state. This ended with me losing my job. I had applied for jobs that I know I was qualified for but never could get one. I was "blackballed" at every turn. I watched people much less qualified get jobs that I applied for. I was always left trying to rationalize why I didn't get the jobs.

I have now moved on, and I don't drive as much as I used to. My life has become much simpler. Since I'm retired, I work when I want to now. I could work every day if I wanted to, but I chose not to. I am at the stage in my life that if I want to work, I can. However, if I don't want to, then I don't have to. There are many people I know who are my age or older who still have to continue to work. A lot of places didn't offer the retirement plan that the school system did.

The years have gone by from the time of my wilderness experience starting until the older lady told me that I was in the wilderness until now. I now have a greater understanding of what had been happening to me over the past forty years. I now realize that I was in a great depression. I lost my joy over this time. I have been happy on many occasions. Happiness is not my joy. Happiness comes and goes according to the situation. Joy is from within.

I have been in crowds of people, and everything is going well, but I didn't have the feeling of joy. I could be laughing and talking, but within, I had that nagging feeling of sadness always lingering. I could watch movies or shows on television and find myself crying when sad things happened to the people in the movies. I've never been a crybaby, and I'm far from a punk, but I guess the depression that I had would just carry me there.

I never considered myself depressed. I just wanted justice served for the past forty years. I had always wanted revenge for the lies that were told on me and the way the school system, court system, lawyers, and judge have mistreated me. The Word of God states, "Vengeance is mine," but I was still trying to get it myself.

There have been many times that people come to me for advice on life's situations, and I have been able to help them through. I have been able to tell them things that have caused them to change their lives. I have been able to tell people things to save their marriage, caused them to regain love and affection from brothers and sisters. I was used to help them bring them back to estranged parents and regain relationships as well as job situations. All the things I've been through have been the catalyst to me being able to do all these things.

However, there have been a lot of situations in my life that I had needed someone to talk to, but I had never found anyone to help me. I have not found anyone that understands what I am saying. In these forty years, I had just learned to keep it to myself. People are always so eager to tell me their problems, but when I wanted to talk, no one wanted to listen. They would start to talk about something else or say they have to leave.

You may not understand this, but in those times, I can now think back and remember hearing in myself God saying, "I am directing you." I now realized what that meant; if I had any problem that I cannot handle, I was to bring it to him. He wanted to answer all our situations and problems. All of my help is in Jesus Christ!

In the last forty years, I have learned that if there is anything that I want in life, I have to ask God. So many times, we want to try to find a person that knows something about the situation or know someone who can help. But now I know that anything that I want or need, I was to come to my Father first, and if I am to have it, he will provide it. Sometimes when we ask God for things, he may say no or we have to wait. We may not be ready for what it is that we are asking for. Other times, God knows better than we do and saw that what we are asking for isn't good for us. We want what we want, but we don't see long-term like he does.

Just to tell you a story…I wanted to refinance my home one time. I talked to this man that worked in that department. He told me that he could do as I asked and that I would receive all this money for free from it. All that I could see was the free money he promised me. God didn't want me to do this, but I was greedy and pushed for it for over a year. God was telling me no because there were negative consequences that would come as a result of me going through with this. Because he loves us, he will allow us sometimes to have what we want that he doesn't want for us. This is called his permissive will. Even though he gave us warning, he will let us have this thing to show us why he was saying no.

So I got the refinance and the "free" money. This was about ten years ago, and I am still dealing with the consequences of that decision. However, what I realize is that I wouldn't be in this situation if I had listened to God all those years ago. I know now that God is with me in small things. The little things in life that happens, God will help us if we just trust him and obey his will. Things that I tell people that God will do, they may not understand or they may even laugh, but I know he will do them!

For the past few years now, I have been telling my wife that something is about to happen for the good in my life. I have been feeling an anxiousness that I cannot explain. It's a good feeling though.

I've had people telling me such things as "God told me to tell you that he has not forgotten you" and "God knows where you are." I have an excitement within me, and I don't know where it comes from or what it is, I just know that it is good!

A minister told me a few months ago that he heard preached a sermon, but he didn't know why. He said that God had given it to him and that it was for someone. He said that he had asked several people in his congregation if it resonated with either of them. They all said no. When I went to see him, he looked at me and said that it was for me. He then went to read the Bible and told me that he had preached on the second chapter of Deuteronomy. He said that things are about to change in my life. I have been in the wilderness but was about to come out!

After that, I talked to a lady from my past that I felt helped to cause my depression. Not that she did anything wrong. It was more that I looked up to her, and I felt that I had let her down along with some other prominent people in my community for losing my job.

I thought that they believed the lie that was told about me when I lost my job.

Well now, forty years later, I am finally talking to this lady concerning that whole situation. In talking to her, she told me that she had been on my side from the beginning. She said that most of the people in the community were on my side and knew that I had not done anything wrong. When she said this to me, I felt 20 pounds lighter. I felt like I could fly! Right on the stop, I felt joy come into my heart. The depression that I had carried for forty years was gone! Life was completely different. I feel like a real man again! I had been wearing a mask all of those years and didn't realize it. Many things had gone on in my life that as I look back now, I sew that because God was with me, they turned out as they did.

That poem about the footprints in the sand have been very true to me, and I didn't realize it. Guess what the real thing that I had learned in these 40 years are? God loves me and will never leave or forsake me! If you develop a relationship with him, he will always be by your side. My forty years were over, and life is getting better, but there's another level God is taking me to now! I know that God's Word is true, and he is going to blow my mind!

About the Author

Walter Bernard Ward Sr. was born June 7, 1952, in Marion, Maryland, in Somerset County to the late Walter and Alma Ward. He was the seventh child out of eleven siblings for which eight are still alive today. Ward grew up and spent most of his life in Somerset County, Maryland. He currently resides in Princess Anne, Maryland, with his wife, Valerie, for which he has been married to for nineteen years, a beautiful, smart, warm, and caring woman. He has two sons (Walter Jr. and Kenneth) and five daughters (Angie, Tanya, LaToya, Antoinette, and Cantrelle) and sixteen grandchildren he enjoys spending time with.

Ward is a lifelong learner, educator, and agent of change and grew up in the era of segregation as a baby boomer. Although the country was embracing the transformation of desegregation, Ward remain focused on achieving his educational goals. He holds a BS degree in Physical Education from Bowie State University, located in

Bowie, Maryland, and a MA degree in Educational Leadership from Salisbury University located in Salisbury, Maryland. Ward has been a member of John Wesley United Methodist Church in Marion, Maryland, for over sixty years. He worked in the education system for over thirty-nine years as both an educator and administrator, vice principal. He retired from the education system in 2010, and today, he spends his days and time traveling, visiting family, and enjoying the finer things in life.

Ward was also the former division I assistant basketball coach at the University of Maryland Eastern Shore in Princess Anne, Maryland, for three seasons from 1987 to 1990 and a baseball, football, basketball, and track coach for forty years at the college, high school and local community levels. Ward was instrumental in winning nine state championships.

Today as a retired educator, Ward's passion and mission is to promote and bring value into the lives of others by "giving back" to his community and the education system. He currently works as a substitute teacher three to four times a week assisting, advising, and helping scholars. Ward's personal relationship with God is evidence of his commitment to be a servant. As an active member of his church, Ward is the president and member of the men's choir, lay pastor and worship leader, usher and chairman of the official board of the church.

Ward's favorite quote is "Never quit, never give up, play to the end." He was led to write a book to share his stories, experiences, *challenges*, and encounters of race, racism, segregation, and desegregation about his life growing up as a boy and young man of color during an era in America that has forever left a mark on his life that cannot be erased and helped him mature into the man he is today.

CPSIA information can be obtained
at www.ICGtesting.com
Printed in the USA
JSHW020213290121
11328JS00001B/10